D0868807

# No Child Held Back:

Creating a New Vision for 21st Century Education Reform

## YOVEL BADASH

ISBN-10: 0615771653
ISBN-13: 978-0-615-77165-6

Library of Congress Cataloging-in-Publication Data
Badash, Yovel.
No child held back: creating a new vision for 21st century education reform / by Yovel Badash.
ISBN 978-0-615-77165-6
1. Education

Editing and design: nLighten, LLC.

Printed in the United States of America

# PRAISE FOR *NO CHILD HELD BACK*

"Finally! A set of practical ideas that flips the No Child Left Behind paradigm on its head with a bold, common sense approach that is long overdue. With refreshing clarity and a great sense of purpose, *No Child Held Back* provides a hard look at a doomed mindset and brightly turns our attention back to our true purposes for education."
—*Victor Rivero, Editor in Chief,* EdTech Digest

"*No Child Held Back* is both a ground-breaking approach to ensuring every child thrives and an idea whose time has come. Using open source technology as its foundation, it opens up a game that allows for all stakeholders in educational transformation to come together as a powerful community, aligned in a common purpose, each contributing their unique and innovative initiatives wherever they can best serve a need." —*Dawnelle Hyland, Award-Winning Educator and CEO, Align Global Leadership*

"First we recognized the need to identify and close gaps. Now visionary author Yovel Badash takes us to the immediate future in which all children don't just meet standards; they soar. Through the eyes of the author we are taken to new places with a new vision for what education could and should be." —*Donna Walker Tileston, Ed.D.*

"*No Child Held Back* captures all the elements of what the optimal education for every child should look like, feel like and be like. No other book has been able to detail every facet of what makes education successful as succinctly as this book has. Its vision will finally propel education into the 21st century. A New Paradigm!" —*Rudy Azcuy, President Teach N' Kids Learn, Inc.*

"Brilliant, timely, and practical, *No Child Held Back* hinges on the not so subtle difference between "left behind" and "held back" indicating a significant change in our mindset regarding education. The book is focused on the critically

*(continued from previous page)*

important element of education, developing teacher effectiveness. The NCHB framework is a technologically-based approach that advocates inspired teaching, community engagement, and personalized student and adult learning. It offers concrete, usable tools that give teachers the power to innovate, create, inspire and thereby optimize learning. Furthermore, NCHB recognizes the power of open-source content and digital learning to fuel the growing need to compete effectively in the global educational forum."
—*Lystra M. Richardson, PhD., Professor, Educational Leadership & Policy Studies, Southern Connecticut State University*

"As I read *No Child Held Back*, I paused at various points to ponder the current state of education. I paused as an educator to consider how we got to this point in which education and politics are so intertwined to the tune of millions and millions dollars. I paused to consider my own children who are in public schools. What pressure do they feel from their teachers? What pressure do I bring to bear upon them as a result of NCLB? Finally, I pause to reflect upon how we, as a community of learners, can transition from NCLB to engage in *No Child Held Back*? After almost 30 years in public education and as the author of numerous articles and five books, I still want to inspire children, parents and peers to love learning. Yovel brings a perspective to NCLB that slowly yet purposefully engages and guides readers to take the next step." —*Hope Blecher, Ed.D.*

# CONTENTS

*"Train up a child according to the tenor of his way*
*and when he is old, he will not depart from it."*
*—said by the Wisest Man in History!*

# ACKNOWLEDGMENTS

**No Child Held** Back is an approach to education that allows every child to thrive. Every child—no matter his or her socioeconomic background, learning style, or life circumstances. This approach was not developed in a vacuum. The world around us has reached an inflection point at which we have sufficient democracy, technological maturity, and global connectivity to deliver all the major elements that will allow us to fulfill this important work.

We build this exciting new framework on the shoulders of all those who came before us having had a marked impact on the quality of our education and our lives—innovators, revolutionaries, leaders, artists, builders, thinkers, dreamers and doers. Indeed, the present and future of education owes a tremendous debt to the past. We could not have reached this point at this time if it weren't for the dedicated efforts of those who came before us, those who led us to where we are today.

While we list out our thanks in a spirit of playfulness, we remain quite serious about our mission to make the highest quality education accessible to all children everywhere—no matter where they may be academically, socioeconomically or geographically.

So, with a light heart but a steadfast mind we thank you, Mark Twain, for lending a sense of humor to the American experience and beyond, and reminding us of the lighter side of things, as you've said, *"I never let my schoolin' get in the way of my learnin'."*

Thank you, Albert Einstein for telling us that *"Imagination is more important than knowledge."*

Thank you Alan Kay, inventor and computer scientist, for guiding us to take charge of our ability to influence the world by telling us, *"The best way to predict the future is to invent it."*

Thank you, Steve Jobs, recently passed, for inspiring us to think differently and merge aesthetics and humanity into technology. You've encouraged us to seize the moment and provided us the tools to do so.

Thank you, François Rabelai, for telling us that, *"A child is not a vase to be filled, but a fire to be lit."*

Thank you, Maria Montessori, for saying so eloquently and with much wisdom, *"Whoever touches the life of the child touches the most sensitive point of a whole which has roots in the most distant past and climbs toward the infinite future."*

Thank you John F. Kennedy for telling us back in 1963 that – *"All of us do not have equal talent, but all of us should have an equal opportunity to develop our talents."*

Thank you, Pablo Casals, for asking great questions, *"And what do we teach our children? We teach them that two and two make four, and that Paris is the capital of France. When will we also teach them what they are?"* We thank you for your wise advice: *"We should say to each of them: Do you know what you are? You are a marvel. You are unique. In all the years that have passed, there has never been another child like you. Your legs, your arms, your clever fingers, the way you move. You may become a Shakespeare, a Michelangelo, a Beethoven. You have the capacity for anything. Yes, you are a marvel."*

We thank all of these great inspirers. We, too, believe that every child is a marvel, a "superkid." We believe that every child has innate talent that, when they can identify and discover it, they will live an inspired purposeful life where they contribute in great measure to the quality of life on our planet. What made Shakespeare *Shakespeare* was a talent identified, accessed, and nurtured. What made Michael Jordan *Michael Jordan* was a talent identified, accessed, and nurtured. While every child may not have her name and gifts known in the public arena—while every child may not be a Shakespeare or a Michael Jordan the capacity for full expression of his or her own talents and the measure of his or her own contribution is just as great in her own sphere of influence.

This simple viewpoint is an amazing game-changer. It is a worldview, an everyday view that assists us in not settling for 'giving it a good try', or merely 'not falling behind'. If we realize that it is up to us—each one of us—to nurture the seed of talent that lies within each child, then we cannot afford to give ourselves any back doors, second chances, or wasted time. On the contrary, we acknowledge that within each moment lies tremendous opportunity for authentic learning, for true magic to happen, and for only the best learning experiences to transpire.

Why *shouldn't* we think this way? Anything short of this mindset is unacceptable. It is a departure from the envisioned state—a state that can be reached through our agreement to make it real.

That said, and a bit closer to our daily work on the NaMaYa team (NaMaYa is a next-generation learning management software provider for the education sector), I would like to pay special thanks to my business partner Eyal for allowing me to focus on what I like to do by dealing with everything else.

Thank you so much Joan, Celine, Eyal, Glenda, Scott, Jennifer, Dylan, Evan and everyone else that is involved in our daily operation. I couldn't have done any of this without your support and faith in our future. You inspire me more than you know!

Thanks also to Victor Rivero, my editor and collaborator, who has made this book possible. Thanks for your insights and contributions in helping to focus my thoughts and for harnessing my energy into something others might venture to read and comprehend.

I feel it is important to also generally acknowledge some of the existing work out there that has directly and indirectly influenced this book. There are a lot of innovative minds moving the education and technology sector forward these days. Thanks to:

- Tom Vander Ark of Getting Smart.com
- Bob Wise of the Alliance for Excellence in Education
- Governor Jeb Bush, Chairman of the Foundation for Excellence in Education
- Mark Weston, co-author along with Alan Bain of the recently published *The Learning Curve*
- Doug Levin, Executive Director of the State Education Technology Directors Association
- Keith Krueger of the Consortium for School Networking
- Milton Chen
- The George Educational Lucas Foundation

- Linda G. Roberts
- Betsy Corcoran of EdSurge
- Yaacov Hecht, founder of the Democratic Education Movement, for teaching us that children have a real voice we should listen to and that we get stronger when we develop our strengths not only our weaknesses
- The New Teacher Project, which is doing groundbreaking work in recruiting and developing teachers who consistently have their students excel
- Achieve, Inc., a bipartisan government commission committed to finding ways to ensure that every student graduates high school with the skills and aptitude to be a contributing citizen as our world evolves.

Of equal importance to the heroes who are working on behalf of quality education at national or international levels are the everyday heroes in our own homes: our parents. Parents, often your hard work to both provide for your families and open up a world of possibilities for your children goes unnoticed. Your children didn't come with manuals on how to raise them, and what teaching and learning looks like in school today is often vastly different than what you experienced. Thank you for your unwavering commitment to your children amid a world of constant changes. Thank you for having the kind of care for the future of your children and *all* children that would cause you to pick up this book. What I want you to know is that you are not alone. Like you, there are many parents reading this who are looking at how they can enable their children to thrive. You are part of an emerging community here, and together, we can all make a marked difference on the future of our education, and through that, the future of our world!

Finally, I want to thank our teachers. What I have seen in all the teachers that I have had the privilege to experience and talk with is that your work is not a job—it is a vocation, a calling. Day in and day out, you seek to do the very best for the children you serve, often with limited resources, having to draw on your own finances and sheer will. While this is honorable, I realize that it is high time that we, as a society, support you in full measure. You are one of my key inspirations behind this book and this NCHB approach. You are the ones responsible for shaping the future of society by helping children to reach their full potential and fulfill their purposes in life. You are the ones who do shape the world, in big and small ways. I am here for you, and this vision, approach, and community that we are growing into together is here for you. NCHB is a rich foundation for you to gain the resources you need to do the important work of nurturing the seed of talent that exists within every child. It is a powerful community where your voice matters.

The vision offered in this book is not finished and will be ongoing for years to come, but let this be more than a mere start. Let us all come together and ensure that this is a re-dedication to the efforts and intentions of so many leaders and innovators out there who are aspiring to excellence in education, and are not afraid of a little innovation to get there. As we rapidly move forward on the course to a better education for all, let's ensure we're all on the same page and re-confirm our commitment to the ideals, to the goals and to the road that will get us there. To join the emerging conversation on this game-changing approach and for more information about becoming involved, please visit www.nochildheldback.com.

*—Yovel Badash*
*New York City*
*December 12, 2012*

YOVEL BADASH

# INTRODUCTION:
# SHIFTING THE PARADIGM

**In a progressively** global economy, American students must have every opportunity to reach their fullest potential in order to be competitive. Despite the increasing importance of education, American students' performance has consistently eroded in comparison to their international peers. This must change. Transforming our education system is not just important for individual students, it is crucial for our country's survival.

What if the focus of the education system were to help all children reach their full personal and academic potential, to make sure that no child is held back from optimal achievement?

Consider a shift from No Child *Left Behind* to No Child *Held Back*. The subtle nuance in language marks a *seismic shift in focus*—from a paradigm that focuses on group norms and an approach where every child is expected to learn in the same ways at the same pace—to one that focuses on *each individual student's unique learning needs*. This has wide-reaching implications for teachers, students—and academic achievement levels. New research shows that student-centered, customized learning is the most reliable model for enabling students of all cognitive abilities to achieve academic success.

NCHB embraces a paradigm focused on customized learning that brings out the unique abilities of every child. It recognizes that within this paradigm, there must be a dynamic shift in the way teachers teach, how communities partner with schools and districts, and how schools and districts adopt and adapt technology. Furthermore, exceptional teaching, strong community partnerships, and thoughtful adoption and adaptation of technology rests on key foundations: positive reinforcement, healthy competition, self-paced learning, diverse means for learning, student and parent responsibility, course variety, quality instruction, and growth for students, parents and educators.

How does a school system move from a factory school approach where "one size fits all" to student-centered, customized learning programs?

The initial step is *transforming the mindset of the educational approach*. A framework based on institutionalizing encouragement, positive reinforcement, and the promotion of healthy competitiveness is critical to creating a culture of excellence. Actively involving the community as a supporting partner and providing parents with actionable means to assist their children extends the approach to important stakeholders beyond the schoolyard boundary.

The second step is to *systematically customize the learning experience*. From matching teaching modalities to each student's optimum learning pattern, to customizing curriculum that keeps students on track, NCHB embraces new ways of engaging students in active learning.

This second step requires that a classroom teacher's role evolve. When teaching modalities match students' learning patterns and curriculum is customized to meet a child where he is, a teacher's work shifts from *imparting* and *assessing* a child's acquisition of knowledge and skills to *facilitating* a child's learning process for optimal achievement.

This is why the core of NCHB is making sure every child has access to great teachers. Great teachers become great by continuing to learn and grow themselves, far beyond their formal years in college. Strong professional development programs empower classroom teachers with advanced skills for individual assessment, one-on-one coaching, and developmental guidance. Because technology can deliver outstanding instructional lectures and related content to any classroom, library, or home—classroom teachers can spend more time nurturing and guiding students and less time on simple content delivery.

It is time to put education back in the hands of teachers, students, parents, and the community—not tests. NCHB offers a viable system that fosters healthy competition, intrinsic motivation, intellectual growth, and academic excellence to every student in every school district in America.

\* \* \*

**As we prepare** our children for life in the globally competitive information age of the twenty-first century, excellence in education is more crucial now than ever before for achieving individual and societal success.

Parents, educators, business leaders, and politicians alike call for improvements in education. In the U.S., public spending increased by 73 percent per student in real-dollar terms since 1970, and student-to-teacher ratios were substantially reduced between 1980 and 2005.

Despite these measures, student achievement remained essentially flat throughout the same period, and American student performance in comparison to the performance scores of students from other countries has consistently and substantially eroded.

In a legislative effort to combat this trend, Congress passed the No Child Left Behind Act of 2001(NCLB), which took effect in 2003. This legislation requires states to establish universal standards for all students, and to regularly administer standardized tests meant to measure student achievement levels. NCLB further mandates that 95 percent of students be tested and that all tested students must achieve state-defined proficiency levels by 2014 regardless of their cognitive or English language abilities. In the decade since the No Child Left Behind Act (NCLB) was passed to combat poor academic performance, the U.S. educational system has seen a progressive shift toward lower state standards and "teaching to the test" in order for schools to avoid the financially punitive measures of the act.

Under the NCLB approach, schools must also ensure that an increasing percentage of students will meet state guidelines each year, thus demonstrating "adequate yearly progress" in their programs. Schools and districts that fail to substantially and consistently improve test scores face harsh punitive measures and federal funding reductions. Supporters of the act cite improved test scores as evidence that an increased emphasis on teacher and school accountability with standardized measures is beneficial.

The U.S. Department of Education reports that from 2000 to 2005, American nine-year olds showed more improvement in reading scores than in the previous 28 years combined; 13-year-old students earned the highest math scores the test ever recorded. During the same period, achievement gaps between white and minority nine-year olds reached record lows due to increases in the minority students' math and reading scores.

Critics, however, argue these favorable statistics are misleading. Since No Child Left Behind did not take effect until 2003, they contend that only two years' worth of increases can be attributed to NCLB, and that no substantial differences in improvement rates occurred after the legislation took effect.

As the current reauthorization of the Elementary and Secondary Education Act, the No Child Left Behind Act continued the original legislation's explicit prohibition against a nationally defined curriculum. Instead, it simply required states to define their own proficiency standards and applies harsh punitive measures to schools that fail to meet state standards regardless of how actual student achievement levels compare to national performance standards.

A recent EdTrust study highlights the wide disparity between lax state standards and national test standards: 89 percent of Mississippi fourth graders achieved state proficiency levels while only 18 percent of them earned passing proficiency scores on the National Assessment of Educational Progress (NAEP). Similarly, in Oklahoma, 75 percent achieved state proficiency levels with only 29 percent meeting national standards. Missouri specifically *lowered* its traditionally high state standards to facilitate compliance with NCLB.

In 2009, the tides did turn to some degree with the ED Recovery Act included as part of the American Recovery and Reinvestment Act. Under ED Recovery, states are encouraged to comply with a set of national "Common Core" standards as one strong criteria for receiving federal "Race to the Top" educational funding. The Act holds that adhering to national standards is critical for students to graduate high school with the skills and abilities to meet the intellectual demands of adult life. In June 2010, "Common Core" standards were released for mathematics and English language arts. ED Recovery also requires that states increase focus on providing quality professional development opportunities for teachers and principals.

These moves are far more pointed in the direction of an NCHB approach. Yet in practice, adoption of Common Core standards still carries with it the mindset of every student learning at the same pace, in the same way. Also, it ties money directly to groups of students achieving or not achieving core standards, leading to the continued phenomena of "teaching to the test." Finally, while it is valuable to encourage strong professional development, schools and districts often cite lack of time and resources as barriers to offering ongoing training that can have a measured, long-term impact. ED Recovery doesn't appear to offer a viable solution to this issue.

Holding teachers and schools accountable for the results of their teaching programs is an admirable goal, but what is critical to realize is that NCLB, the *legislation*, is the outcropping of an NCLB mindset that simply won't work to ensure that every child thrives. The psyche behind the NCLB paradigm and its Race to the Top successor is fundamentally incompatible with a true quest for educational excellence. These acts' primary focus on delivering uniform education to the general student population, and their application of excessively harsh punishments for failures to push even cognitively and linguistically challenged students to perform at grade-level is flawed. This approach forces educators and administrators to manage programs in a fashion that ensures funding levels—but fails to bring out the best in each student.

Despite all of this, what if the focus of the education system were to help all children reach their full personal and academic potential, and to make sure that no child is held back from optimal achievement? What if this was not a dim dream, rather a vision that anyone and everyone began taking practical action to actually realize? What if optimal achievement for every student became our reality?

Toward that end, this book is not simply a philosophical read but a call to action and a workbook for students, teachers, parents, administrators, business leaders and others in and around education who believe in improving the current state of affairs.

In other words, the hard—and rewarding—work starts now. There are no shortcuts, no silver bullets. Turn back now if you dread responsibility. This book will *involve* you in change, not simply provide a platform to share ideas. If you have read this far, it is clear that you really want to make a difference.

Sit alone with this book; think, reflect, and be inspired.

The chapters are organized by three categories:

*Why*. Use these chapters to re-connect with what is truly at stake in all of our lives as we consider the next evolution of our education systems around the world.

*What*. Use these chapters to understand the NCHB framework and consider its implications for you and your community.

*How*. Use these chapters to inform yourself of tools and resources available for supporting every child in succeeding, as well as to be inspired by practitioners who have already begun to realize the NCHB vision.

Throughout each chapter, you will learn of people and organizations who have embraced the NCHB vision successfully. We invite you to explore deeply what they are doing. Recognize that those who embrace this vision are working together as part of an emerging global community committed to the success of every child.

Use the questions at the end of each chapter to connect with the ideas personally, and apply them in ways that are relevant to your own educational community.

And, as the ideas, stories, and questions begin to help you develop your own full vision in your sphere of influence—then, by all means, take action! Chapter 14 will support you in doing just that. In addition, I've included "Talking Points" at the end of each chapter that will provide guidance for you as you move to enroll those within your sphere of influence to put this NCHB vision into practice.

No matter how small the step, with small successes, you can expand outward and upward and lead others in a desirable direction as well. And, chances are, before you know it, people will be coming to you for help. This book is dedicated to making a difference and, more importantly, to those who would become the difference-makers. *That's you!*

YOVEL BADASH

# *Why*

**Before undertaking any** intentional move to transform our schools, it is imperative to understand *why* it matters to do so. After all, it takes time, dedication, commitment, a willingness to engage in dialogue, and a willingness to 'stay the course' in the face of those individuals in whom such a mindset may not catch hold right away, or bureaucratic policies that would be roadblocks.

The recently released film *Won't Back Down* highlights the reform journey of a teacher, Nona Alberts and parent, Jamie, committed to transforming their failing school to a place of engaged, successful learning for every child. They met with all kinds of opposition along the way: colleagues who, while they knew things weren't working, were comfortable with the status quo; a system of policies that, initially, produced a barrier to moving ahead with a powerful learning program; and the interests of unions that wanted things to remain the same.

A general recognition that may sound in your mind something like *"oh, of course we need to reform our schools"* may not be enough to have you continue to live the vision, day in and day out. Nona and Jamie had to be in touch with what was at stake.

These next three chapters provide you with a picture of what is at stake. They also offer a view of how the culture of learning has been evolving to bring us to a point where education reform to the tune of a NCHB approach is exactly what is needed. In these chapters, you will learn that NCHB is indeed an idea whose time has come.

YOVEL BADASH

# 1
# THE POWER OF EDUCATION IN DAILY LIFE

**For better or** for worse, *everything* is tied to education: violence, crime, intolerance, war, poverty, racism, classism, sexism—as well as civil discourse, contribution, tolerance, peace, affluence, understanding among cultures and ethnic groups, opportunity, harmony, and robust economic health. The power of education plays a role in each and every person's life on a very personal level, and expands outward to a family level and then on to social and professional groups, teams, associations, companies and further on to local, state, national and international levels. It isn't too difficult to make the connection: the quality of a nation's education can and does ultimately sway its Gross Domestic Product (GDP).

Education is, in fact, what has made our society flourish and grow. Whenever and wherever there have been advances in civilization, they were preceded by a period where a strong value was placed on education. Witness the Age of Reason, the Enlightenment, the Reformation. Each new enlightened age produced milestone achievements. From mapmaking and the printing press to automobiles and commercial flight, education was a central element.

Education is the key for personal and community growth; there is nothing more important we can do than to focus on providing the very best educational system possible. However, unless this system is applied to something, unless the theory of education is then manifested in the real world—or quite simply, unless what you learn is put into practice—no matter how perfectly or sloppily it is done—then real change will remain just a dim dream and not an actual reality.

As a democratic society, we may fight about healthcare, about the military budget or about social security—but the best way for us to have real influence is by creating higher quality, less expensive and widely accessible education for every student everywhere. If we were to ensure that every student is truly learning and able to contribute their talents and gifts to our communities, it may be observed that the national GDP would consequently rise.

We are living in a digital age in an increasingly global economy. Yet, while strides have been made, our educational system is still largely in a factory-model mindset where every child moves one year to the next from kindergarten through grade 12, from classroom to classroom, expected to master a certain body of material within a year's time in the same ways that the rest of their peers are learning. Schools and districts are expected to innovate, diversify to meet the needs of various learning styles and provide robust learning experiences for both students and teachers all too often with a few computers per classroom, and in buildings with overcrowded classrooms that can't accommodate a growing population. This isn't working. We simply must create new systems of education to keep pace with the radical changes in our world.

Let's look at keeping pace from a financial standpoint.

Education has always been the ultimate equalizer. Throughout history, the wealthy and the aristocracy preserved their class through education. Rich people have more money to *buy* education for their children and wealthier countries tend to earmark more money toward offering high quality education to those members of society it values.

As things currently stand, it's very difficult to afford the entire educational process, from pre-Kindergarten through college. The cost of education juxtaposed with salary percentages has only increased out of proportion to everything else. According to a report issued jointly by the American Council on Education and the Council for the Advancement and Support of Education, rising college tuition costs have had to be put into place to offset reductions in state revenues. In 1980, states provided 46% of the operating support for public colleges and universities. By 2005, that amount had fallen to 27%. During that same time, tuition as a source of revenue increased from 13 to 18%.

These are clear indications that education has become *too expensive*. It is estimated that the average cost per student per year in public school is about $11,000; that means that a K-12 education for one child in a public system costs the government $143,000; in a private school, this cost is assumed by parents. Areas in the U.S. that are notably "lower income" don't have the tax brackets to support the rising costs of education. As a result, in these districts students get sub-standard and archaic learning materials ("hand me downs" from other, wealthier districts that have adopted new textbooks or technology) and larger class sizes.

At the college level, earning a bachelor and graduate degree can cost a family between $40,000 - $300,000 for six years. When these degrees are obtained through public universities, state and federal monies subsidize the cost at about the same level of spending per student.

If we are thinking about a world where we are truly free and equal, then *everyone* should have the right to the best education *regardless* of how much money their parents have, and regardless of the ability of their home state or district to subsidize at high or low levels. If education is the key for each person in reaching their full potential, then it follows that education is not a privilege for the elite few. It is not an expectation for the middle classes of developed countries. Nor is it something that is delivered with quality for the suburban masses and all but abandoned in the "inner cities" of the world.

**In fact, education is a right we must give every child around the world—and it is a fundamental right.**

Let's look at keeping pace from another financial angle. In addition to per student cost for materials and instruction, there are capital development costs to consider.

The National Center for Education Statistics reports that "dramatic increases in enrollment due to the 'babyboom echo,' migration, and immigration have led schools to enroll far more students than they were designed to accommodate." In addition, it reports that the school-aged population has reached an all-time high at 55 million students, and that the size of the student body will almost double by 2100.

If we are looking at global population growth and juxtaposing that with elementary, high school, postsecondary college or university levels, then there is a real chance that our current physical institutions will not be able to sustain a fully literate humanity. The population growth would make higher education, whether it is university, college, or trade school, rare. We cannot continue to view education in traditional ways – sitting in a classroom listening to one teacher. *Where* would everyone sit? We would need to open a new school or new university every week in order to support the population growth. In fact, in many districts around the country, trailers are being added to brand new schools before the doors even open.

It is time to transcend the boundaries of brick and mortar schools by thinking in new ways about how to provide high-quality, cost - effective education. As we delve more deeply into the digital age in an ever-increasing global economy with more human beings on the planet, we simply have no choice but to *evolve our education* in order to keep pace.

So, how do we go about ensuring that every child, regardless of where they grow up or their socioeconomic status, has access to a quality education in the midst of ever-rising costs and a rapidly growing population?

Consider these two possibilities:

## 1. Use of Technology

Think about how much money could be saved if educational institutions adopted more technology. Used in the right ways and with proper training, technology can become our modern day equalizer.

Technology is flexible and fluid, and we should be able to use it to educate all children more effectively, dynamically, and *differently*, providing them with what they need to succeed in today's world—rather than the world of yesteryear.

Case in point: not so long ago, the focus in education was strictly on acquiring information—facts, statistics, events. Moreover, there was no way for you to get information unless you picked up the phone or made a trip to the library, the mailbox, the museum or the university. Professors, teachers and others used to teach with an encyclopedia or a library. Finally, information available was confined to a single source or two.

This is no longer how our world functions, nor are the skills of the past the same skills needed today. In the twenty-first century, Twitter, Facebook, Google, YouTube, and the like make multiple sources of information available—literally at a child's fingertips. And thriving as a global citizen is not just about learning information—it's about being able to access information, review multiple perspectives on a single topic with a thoughtful and discerning eye, synthesize it, and apply it to daily concerns and to create new solutions and opportunities.

Paid, low-cost and free online resources such as the University of Phoenix (UOP), Straighterline, Udacity and Khan Academy are widely available, making acquiring the necessary skills to facilitate learning for all students possible. Massively Open Online Courses (MOOCs) are just now beginning to disrupt old-school, calcified models of learning.

On an interesting personal note, I earned my degree and finished with honors at a University of Phoenix-like university—the Open

University in Israel. I chose to earn it that way for multiple reasons. First, it fit my personality, and I could do it on my own time by myself. Secondly, it enabled me to work and advance my career while also figuring out my career path. I was able to finish a computer science and management degree, and I earned it faster, after hours and at my own convenience. That's when I realized the seed of No Child Held Back: *why isn't this opportunity available to everyone?* I thought to myself.

In the early stages of online education, people questioned its validity. As with most seismic changes, people called it into question and challenged its quality. Today, when someone earns their degree online, there is a different association attached to it. It's no longer sketchy or cheap. It's that a motivated professional decided to walk the extra mile, demonstrating great strength, discipline and a leading-edge attitude. An online degree can mean that you're an executive from a large company with a busy schedule who needed to round out your professional development and took the initiative to do so on your own schedule. You got things done.

Those who would argue to maintain an era of brick-and-mortar learning espouse the benefits of elite membership to social clubs and associations such as the Harvard Club or those from other Ivy League schools. Many of these associations still have a building where graduates gather. For instance, the physical place that is the Harvard Club in Manhattan.

However, what are they all—but *social networks?* And what age are we living in but an age of social networking? All of these clubs were managed with the technologies and in the circumstances of their time.

The circumstances of our time require that we think and act differently about how we all learn and grow together.

This brings us to the second factor to consider in making a quality education available to every child and, in doing so, to increasing the forward progress of our world.

## 2. Personal Responsibility

Nothing happens without belief. All the technology in the world won't make much of a difference if you don't *believe* that each child can and will excel.

It is each individual's responsibility to believe that the reality of the highest-quality education for all—no matter their circumstances, is possible. Whether you are a teacher, student, administrator, parent, or concerned citizen, you are a stakeholder in educational reform. This belief in every child thriving is fundamental to success. That is to say, when No Child Held Back is made a reality, it will have been made so only by *your belief* that it could truly happen—combined with your dedicated efforts. There cannot be any other way. We must do this; we must have the reality that everyone has this chance for the best education.

More than a few people have overcome formidable obstacles to rise to great heights. Cut from his high school basketball team as a sophomore, Michael Jordan continued to practice his shooting for hours on end and went on to become a star athlete. Barack Obama, the son of a single mom and raised partly by his grandparents, went on to become President. Oprah Winfrey grew up with very little means and in a poor community. She also dealt with personal trauma early in her life. She states over and over that education allowed her to design and live a purpose-filled life. Actor Robin Williams and actress Whoopi Goldberg; boxing great Muhammad Ali; Presidents George Washington and Woodrow Wilson and auto innovator Henry Ford all had dyslexia, a learning condition that makes reading difficult. All of these public figures and many more were able to find ways to learn that worked for them, and they excelled—despite their circumstances.

So it's not the external conditions that make success possible. It's the belief that *every* child can thrive. From that belief, resources and approaches appear in ways that wouldn't be seen otherwise.

Making education a priority and a success is in our hands. How far one goes in life is ultimately up to the individual—our collective belief in optimal achievement for every child provides the context for individuals aspiring to greatness.

Why are you reading this book? The power of education in your own daily life is important to you. No doubt you are a change agent of some sort: a leader, a person who is reaching out to take action and to become the change in your community that you wish to see, to paraphrase Gandhi.

In fact, everyone can become the change they wish to see in the world—and this book, along with the NCHB resources and emerging community—will help inspire and guide you to make it happen. Learn more at www.nochildheldback.com

We need to further strengthen the importance of education. You can help. Join the conversation and take action.

We can agree that on many levels our "world is flat" and yes, everyone is 'competing' with one another; but at the end of the day, *we all benefit* from a quality education. If education is better, then everyone benefits. There's more commerce, more innovation, more business, more production, more new schools, and together, with increased student achievement for everyone, we can accomplish a lot more as a society. *Everyone* will gain from having better education.

# NO CHILD HELD BACK

## For Your Consideration

1. Describe how education influences all aspects of our lives. Choose one aspect then compare and contrast how this aspect would change with less education and with more education.
2. Name the people that you do or can have influence on with regard to education.
3. Describe how each person is ultimately responsible for how much education he or she receives.
4. Write your own vision of how education can be made available to anyone at an affordable price. How would you accomplish this vision?
5. Envision the advances that our society would make if everyone were well-educated.
6. List three societal concerns that could be eradicated through education.
7. Compare and contrast the methods of teaching and communication of your school years with what is available now.
8. Did you or someone you know earn a degree from an online school? What were the advantages and disadvantages of that decision?
9. Name three things that you can do right now to become more involved in educational reform.

No Child Held Back™

## NOTES

_____

_____

_____

_____

_____

_____

_____

_____

_____

_____

_____

_____

_____

_____

_____

_____

_____

**For Your Exploration**

Do an Internet search of the Age of Reason, the Enlightenment, and the Reformation:

- When were these eras?
- Who were the major influences during these times?
- What advances came out of these periods of history?

Research your local school. How is it reaching beyond the walls of the classrooms?

No Child Held Back™

## NOTES

_____

_____

_____

_____

_____

_____

_____

_____

_____

_____

_____

_____

_____

_____

_____

_____

_____

_____

## Talking Points

1. The quality of a country's education has a direct impact on its citizens' quality of life.

For example, when students are not given an environment that meets their learning needs and allows them to tap into their passions, they'll often get bored, and in some cases, drop out. These students are not equipped to contribute to their communities, and they are not fulfilled. In multiple studies and reports, crime rates have been directly correlated with high school drop-out rates and low self-esteem, which often links back to a human being not feeling useful. Consider this: the government plans prison capacity based on third-grade reading results. Hard to believe, but it's true! When a child can't read by the end of the third grade, it affects the government prison capacity planning for the future. Every time our system doesn't support a child in receiving a quality education, society pays a very high long-term price: higher crime rates, more money needed to build and maintain prisons, lower GDP and overall market productivity, less innovation, and higher unemployment, to name a few.

2. Our world is shifting, and we must have an education system that allows children to thrive in the 21st century.

We no longer live in a "one source" world, a world where our access to information is limited to an encyclopedia or whatever books the library happens to carry. All of us have access to countless sources of information. To succeed in the modern world, students must be able to think critically and discern between the wide array of information available. They also must know how to participate in a global economy, and contribute their own unique perspectives and talents to the wide and deep bank of emerging knowledge. The No Child Held Back approach, which becomes manifest through open source technology, allows for students to learn in ways that will allow them to thrive in today's world.

3. Technology is a way of life in the 21$^{st}$ century, and provides a solution to the escalating costs of education and the "digital divide" between communities in high and low-income tax brackets.

Textbooks cost money. School buildings cost money. Teacher salaries cost money. Teacher preparation and professional development costs money. Running a school costs money. As the population grows, the need for these resources grow. As unemployment rises, money from state and federal taxes to fund public school decreases. An education system based on effective use of technology offers a low-cost way to provide high-quality education to every child, everywhere.

Case in point: Mooresville Graded School District (MGSD) in Mooresville, NC. A rural district in a low income area, MGSD undertook a digital conversion from 2009 to 2012. The average cost per student and teacher per year to receive laptops and a data bank of customizable content is about $184.50 per person. Prior to the conversion, they paid between $30 and $89 for *one* textbook for *one* child. At the minimum end of this range, the cost of educating a high school student on a blocked schedule of four classes per day per semester is $120. Add the second semester, and the cost rises to $240. The cost of high-quality professional development from an expert provider for one teacher for one day is minimally $150. In a district with 450 teachers, this equates to $67,500. This same high-quality professional development is available to teachers through a customized content pool of modules and courses, where principals can self-select what is most needed for their schools, and teachers can self-select courses that will allow them to grow in the areas they've targeted for themselves.

The difference in cost is astounding. By dramatically cutting spending on material resources, the district can allocate more money to helping its teachers become highly effective. A digital conversion of this nature is possible for every school district around the world.

Read more about MSGD: http://www5.mgsd.k12.nc.us/staffsites/ digitalconversion/Digital Conversion// MGSD Digital Conversion.html

No Child Held Back™

NOTES

_____

_____

_____

_____

_____

_____

_____

_____

_____

_____

_____

_____

_____

_____

_____

_____

_____

_____

No Child Held Back™

## NOTES

_____

_____

_____

_____

_____

_____

_____

_____

_____

_____

_____

_____

_____

_____

_____

_____

YOVEL BADASH

# 2
# REVISITING THE ROLE OF THE EDUCATION SYSTEM

**In the last** chapter, we saw how education must keep pace with an ever-increasing digital world in a global economy. Under a new paradigm, the role of education must change.

Whether it takes the name of the education law in the U.S. or not – the current education system (all over the world) works under the No Child Left Behind (NCLB) vision and mindset. So *what is* the vision of NCLB? Let's look at the paradigm we are currently in.

When NCLB came into action, its intention was to ensure that each student throughout the U.S. was meeting minimum requirements through standardized testing. This view fails to acknowledge a student who may need to review a concept a few more times than their peers, or the student who gets a concept the first time they are introduced to it. It ignores the fringes of the bell curve—and instead focuses on making everyone conform to the cookie-cutter mold set forth by the average students. Because there are more students that are "average," as indicated by the testing, efforts are focused on getting those students to the next level. Below-average students are not ready to move on to the next level; above average students are already on it. Under this system, the "average" student is more of a concept, rather than a real indication of a child's ability level. It is a norming term that groups kids together under a label rather than looking at their individual capabilities. When you are trying not to leave anyone behind and focused on a romanticized ideal of "average," you end up pushing "average" and "below-average" students back and holding back students in front. Therefore, students are held back, trapped in mediocrity, or left behind.

Picture what it would be like if *everyone* were allowed to advance to the next level at their appropriate time, in a way that honored their individual aptitudes, learning styles, and capabilities.

Every successful company has a vision. Individuals even establish visions. Why? Because visions are basically dreams of the potential of something, how we would love for something to be. Without a vision, how does one know where he or she is going? How does one know what he is reaching for? Dreams drive us to act. They are the fuel that feeds the fire.

The vision of No Child Left Behind is to improve education by "setting high standards" that are then tested through "measurable outcomes." But these standards are high for whom? Every student is different. "High" is a relative and highly interpretive term. "High" for some may seem easy—while seemingly unachievable for others. This view assumes every student is the same, which is simply not true.

## Deconstructing the concept of "no child left behind"
Let's take a look at what "no child left behind" means in a literal sense. It implies that no one can move forward until everyone is on the same page, or at least passes tests adequately. It means that students who could otherwise accelerate at a quick pace are left bogged down waiting for those who are slower. It means those who are slower feel too much pressure to catch up by learning just enough to pass a test but are not truly learning the concepts.

## The factory approach to education—and why it doesn't work
This current approach to education under the NCLB vision is like that of a factory: use mold A, put in plastic B, and get widget C. Bing, bang, boom. Easy-peasy. But the reality is that school is *not* a factory where widgets are made. It's a place where minds of living people are shaped—people of all races, socio-economic groups,

viewpoints, styles, and backgrounds. The view is that people should conform to school, and that they should do as they are told.

## Penalty-based model

Standardized tests, in their current iteration, add fuel to the fire of the "one size fits all approach." One of the biggest points of public contention with NCLB is that it penalizes schools for "poor performance" as indicated by standardized tests. This is a fear-based approach to getting schools to comply with certain provisions, and it is unworkable. For example, in some U.S. locations, an entire school is restructured if it does not hit its NCLB target testing score goals. This means that most or all of the staff are replaced and students are required to attend class for longer periods of time. If this still fails, the school may be closed. But what if the school is teaching their students well in topics that are not tested, thereby resulting in "failure"? What if the school is dealing with other issues that are preventing it from delivering effective education? The scope of how students and schools are judged is far too narrow.

## Fundamental Flaws in the NCLB Approach

As we analyze the logic and structure of NCLB, we find it simply won't work for the world we live in. Here's why:

**It Ignores Aptitude.** Students are individuals, and individuals are naturally different from one another, each with a different learning style and different learning pace. Each person has his or her own ability to advance and a unique speed of progress. The demands of No Child Left Behind limit learning opportunities for both average and above-average students by not acknowledging that some students learn at a different pace than others.

**It Standardizes Academic Weakness.** No Child Left Behind inadvertently weakens schools as states set lower standards for testing in order to comply with these new regulatory provisions. When an entire state measures its students against low performance standards, it is easy to become deluded that academic improvements are being accomplished since other schools in the peer group are also performing against the same poor standard.

Setting the bar low allows the slowest students to keep up; however, a top-performing school in a state with lax standards still leaves students at a serious disadvantage in the face of global competition.

**It Narrows Curriculum.** Because of the high stakes associated with standardized tests under NCLB, many educators and school districts have been accused of "teaching to the test"— reallocating instruction time to teach testing strategies and narrowly focusing teaching concepts to repetitively cover likely test material rather than teaching a broad body of knowledge. Also, greater emphasis on core classes means less time for other subjects. A recent report from the Center for Education Policy found that a significant number of school districts have reduced instructional time for subjects not covered by standardized tests in order to spend more time on reading, language arts, and math. Among these districts, 27 percent have reduced instructional time for social studies, 22 percent for science, 20 percent for art and music, 10 percent for physical education, and 18 percent for other subjects.

**It Ignores Gifted Students.** No Child Left Behind makes no provision for gifted students. It has no special programs to encourage talented students and no penalties for ignoring their unique needs. While the U.S. spends more than $8 billion on special education for mentally disadvantaged students, less than $800 million is devoted to the needs of gifted and talented students. In its August 16, 2007 article "Are We Failing Our Geniuses?", *TIME* Magazine reports, "The year after the President signed the [NCLB] law in 2002, Illinois cut $16 million from gifted education; Michigan cut funding from $5 million to $500,000. Federal spending declined from $11.3 million in 2002 to $7.6 million [in 2007]."

Given these budget limitations, it is critical to find ways to deliver programs that challenge and engage gifted students within the existing cost structure of regular educational delivery.

Even more damaging than the lack of spending allocation for gifted programs is NCLB's diversion of teacher and administrative attention to the needs of the lowest quartiles of students and away from the needs of the highest quartile of students. While these students may easily attain minimum state competency levels with no special accommodation and minimal resource allocation, they will never live up to their true potential without the nurturing and guidance of fully engaged teachers. Failing to fully engage these students creates an irreversible and incalculable loss to our country's global competitiveness, to each student's future, and to our society as a whole.

Despite these numerous failings and a growing number of reform movements, No Child Left Behind will continue to be a federal law for the foreseeable future unless we make a dramatic shift. Educators and administrators must continue to meet its requirements or risk losing funding for their schools.

Yet, there is another, viable possibility. The possibility of No Child Held Back. *What is the thinking driving No Child Held Back?*

**'Real learning for all' is the most important thing.** Education is fundamental for everyone. In fact, we should say it is a fundamental right. And, unlike NCLB may lead us to believe, education is not just knowledge. Education provides the foundation upon which new and exciting inventions and advancements can be created. It can spark new thought, new ideas, new points of view. Education is only taken in if students are open to receive it, if *they want* to receive it. What's the best way to do that? Excite them, help them feel accomplished, help them reach goals based on their abilities—and not standardized tests. Make the materials interesting and relevant to them. Provide them with basic knowledge, but also let them take the reins a bit while still guiding them. Teach them how they learn best, whether that be kinesthetically, visually, tactilely, linguistically, auditorily, or in a combination of learning styles.

**Rather than asking students to conform to their school,** what about taking the alternate viewpoint and, *setting a school up to conform to the needs of its students?* Obviously, in current school settings this wouldn't work. One teacher ends up with a classroom of 25, and, in some parts of our country and world, as many as 50. Without resources and new methodologies, this teacher is left to the old model of teaching in one way for 25-50 different individuals. So the way the system is currently set up is a great disadvantage to each of the students. Some students perform better by being hands on rather than sitting still for hours on end. This is typically true of boys; they have more energy than girls and crave hands-on learning.

Others need to sit quietly and consider concepts before feeling confident to move forward.

Any 21st-century aware citizen can understand that technology, coupled with other teaching methodologies and modes, can become our modern-day equalizer. The beauty of a 'digital' education is that it can conform to each student, whatever his or her specific needs are. Yes, this would take the development of a variety of different curricula based on learning styles that could then be utilized by each student through digital means. However, this is not as far out of the realm of possibility as you might think.

Consider this: In 2010, McKinsey & Company compiled a report entitled "How the World's Most Improved Systems Keep Getting Better," in which commonalities among schools around the globe were examined. The report addresses the best steps, as proven through already improved schools, for moving a school from poor to great. It offers a tiered approach, allowing schools to define where they are on a sliding scale of "poor" to "great" and make steady progress to high achievement for every student regardless of culture or location.

The schools with the most improvement took steps along the scale. Depending on where they were, they moved from poor to fair, fair to good, good to great, and/or great to excellent.

Within each step, schools focused on different aspects of setting themselves up to win. For example, schools that went from poor to fair focused on establishing the organization, finances and pedagogy; while schools moving from good to great focused on shaping the requirements and practices for teachers.

From these patterns it was concluded that schools would do well to follow the journey of schools with similar journeys to their own—rather than trying to emulate those that are significantly different.

The report also addresses that schools can improve from wherever they are—whether a school self-assessed its current condition as poor, fair or good. It also shows that they can improve quickly. The report gives examples of schools in India, Brazil and South Africa in which literacy and numeracy rates have significantly improved within just two to four years. Another example cited is a set of schools in Long Beach, Calif., where six years of interventions increased student performance in grades four and five math by 50 percent and 75 percent respectively.

Also according to this report, there are three primary types of interventions: structural, process-focused and resource-focused. Although improvement can be made from all three types, the vast majority of schools with improvement focused on changing how content is delivered by teachers rather than the content itself.

The complete report can be found at www.mckinseyonsociety.com under "Education."

With a strong focus on technology, No Child Held Back utilizes these findings and establishes suggested steps for implementing a new program no matter where a school is on the scale, rather than trying to fit one program to every school. It also suggests that schools can make improvements quickly.

Now, I am not saying that all of this can be accomplished overnight. It can't. There are the issues of infrastructure as well as current misconceptions about how students should be taught.

However, if you take a step back and look at the big picture, is it not strange that we teach our students with the viewpoint that we all learn the same content in the same ways based solely on our ages? *Why should a highly intelligent nine-year-old be expected to remain in a class just because others are of his or her age?* With NCHB, a student can socially be with his or her peers while at the same time pursuing knowledge at a higher level. How is that possible with only one teacher? Why are we thinking that it's okay for our students to learn a subject from only one teacher when they could have many and could have access to a much broader base of knowledge? By giving technology a bigger role in education, we would be broadening the horizons of all students.

Even when we get to college, we are expected to sit in a giant auditorium with one tenured professor reciting lectures he's given a thousand times without once making eye contact with any student. Perhaps this seems like an extreme example, but it is true of many larger universities, especially in many of the general education classes required in the first two years of undergraduate studies. Why would we or should we listen to just one person when we can have access to many? If we can't get an answer to our question from one teacher, we should be able to go to another.

Students no longer have to settle for this strange and archaic form of education. They can have access to the very best education from anywhere in the world through on-demand, open-source technology, customized to them and their individual needs.

## The No Child Held Back vision

So, *what is* the No Child Held Back vision? It is providing access to an educational web of the best knowledge on the planet in a format that best suits the individual needs of each student while encouraging the achievement of certain goals and rewarding those goals. It is a promise that every child is given the opportunity to develop his or her full range of unique talents, abilities, and gifts. How fun, how individualized; *how possible*.

With the implementation of the Internet, we are getting smarter. Or perhaps I should say *savvier*. We're getting savvier at cutting through the PR of companies telling us one thing and being able to see what the reality is by being able to communicate with others – on a global scale. This only used to be possible through word-of-mouth and usually only through our friends. We now have the resources to be more thoughtful, more discerning of what we're being told versus accepting information blindly. And as it is true in the world of business, so it is with the educational system. We're seeing more and more easily what is working and what is not.

## Time to act

Now is the time to change the fledgling system. Never before in the history of mankind have we ever had so much access to so much knowledge in our hands. Never have we been able to connect to others so easily no matter where we are in the world. Never have we been able to gain answers so quickly to our questions. Technology and the Internet have provided us with the opportunity to provide student-focused, student motivated education – anywhere.

Looking back over the last two hundred years, education hasn't changed too much. We are still operating within a system that worked during a time where students were groomed primarily to help harvest the family farm or run the town store, and an Industrial Age that prepared students to work in factories. The iconic schoolhouse model simply won't work for today's circumstances. We simply can't keep moving on that track.

Without a drastic shift in the way the entire educational system works, we will continue to turn out students who are ill-equipped to keep pace with a rapidly and ever-changing global society. Generations of ill-equipped students lead to higher crime rates, falling economies and, perhaps even most importantly, a squashing of the creative spirit that lives in each one of us and says, *"I want to matter."* This simply cannot continue. We have no more room to let any of our precious students fall through the cracks. No Child Held Back is an idea whose time *has* come—an idea that is, some would even say, *long overdue.*

It's time to shift our focus to what we can do to nurture the seeds of greatness in every child and, in doing so, to create a thriving, more just world where prosperity and true fulfillment can occur for everyone.

## For Your Consideration

1. How would you define education? What makes an education good or poor? Do you believe that there can be a perfect education?

2. What is your vision for education within your sphere of influence?

3. Name some ways to motivate students to learn.

4. Name some ways that students become discouraged during their educational journey.

5. Give some possible reasons why students would not be engaged in learning.

6. How can teachers, parents, and others engage students in learning?

7. What are some steps that you can take to influence educational reform?

8. List some ways that students can be rewarded for accomplishing educational goals.

9. If classes were not based on age, on what would they be based?

10. Do you think that it is important to keep students with their peer groups? What are some ways that students can socialize with other peer groups?

11. In what ways does the current educational system limit a student's access to information?

12. Think about what subjects your state tests. What other subjects do you feel are equally important but not emphasized?

13. What happens to gifted students as individuals when they are held back?

14. What happens to special needs students as individuals when they are left behind?

No Child Held Back ™

**NOTES**

_____

_____

_____

_____

_____

_____

_____

_____

_____

_____

_____

_____

## For Your Exploration

1. Read *"How the World's Most Improved School Systems Keep Getting Better"* by McKinsey & Company. Describe stage-dependent interventions. Describe cross-stage interventions.

Reflect: What stage best defines the school that you teach in or administer at, and/or most directly impacts your child and your community?


2. Read *Hooray for Diffendoofer Day* by Dr. Seuss. How does this book apply to standardized testing and choosing content to be taught in a classroom?

No Child Held Back
™

## NOTES

_____

_____

_____

_____

_____

_____

_____

_____

_____

_____

_____

_____

_____

_____

_____

_____

_____

_____

## Talking Points

1. No Child Left Behind is not just a law—it's a mindset; an approach. Under the mindset, schools are penalized or rewarded based on performance scores of groups of students. This keeps the focus on moving a group forward, and ignores the needs of individuals.

In practice, NCLB assumes that every child learns the same way at the same pace, making little room for learning customization—customization of content or of the learning process. This keeps too many students from achieving their greatest potential.

It also suggests that the role of a teacher is to impart information and craft learning experiences for students. This puts the monkey on the teachers' back, so to speak, rather than giving students the responsibility of finding what interests them and what works for them and pursuing it.

2. No Child Held Back is a mindset that allows every child to develop his or her full range of unique talents, abilities, and gifts.

Under the NCHB approach, students and teachers have access to a wide range of high-quality content and are able to customize the learning process in formats that suit the individual needs of each student.

Under this approach, a teacher's role is to facilitate learning, and a student has far greater responsibility and power to chart a course for an educational journey that works for him or her.

No Child Held Back

## NOTES

_____

_____

_____

_____

_____

_____

_____

_____

_____

_____

_____

_____

_____

_____

_____

_____

_____

_____

# YOVEL BADASH

# 3
# WHY EDUCATION REFORM
# IS NEEDED NOW

**Education reform is** nothing new to the 20th century. In fact, it's been a subject of discourse for thousands of years since formal education became relevant during the ancient Greek and Roman Empire. Leaders throughout history have debated what subjects and practices will lead to well-educated individuals and, ultimately, an educated and prosperous society.

From John Dewey and Maria Montessori to Jean-Jacques Rousseau and A. Bronson Alcott, education reformers have always pushed the boundaries and challenged the status quo for something better and more efficient.

**Yesterday vs. today**
The debate about education began as early as Plato when he pointed out the negative side of compulsory learning and instead promoted the philosophy that children would never learn anything unless they wanted to learn.

As time continued, formal education was only available to the very rich who could pay a private tutor. This education was classical in nature and had greater emphasis on history and classical languages like Latin and Greek rather than on current issues of importance.

This led to the further dichotomy between the wealthy and the working class.

Formal education for all became of utmost importance when overall economic conditions improved and public education could be implemented. Early in public education, the Victorians saw the importance of emphasizing timely topics with commercial benefits like modern languages and mathematics in lieu of a classical education.

Though our education system has evolved from age to age, we are still operating under a "one size fits all" approach, as we saw in earlier chapters. We should be asking ourselves how we can change our educational system from a compulsory system with a far too heavy importance on passing tests—to a system that gets students fired up to learn in spite of differences in personality, learning style and interests.

Current trends indicate that our current system will no longer suffice. We've seen alternatives to typical public education like charter schools explode across America. There are currently more than 4,000 charter schools with more than 1.4 million enrolled students. There are also many people who choose to homeschool for purely academic reasons. In the past, people primarily homeschooled for religious reasons; now there are more and more groups of homeschoolers that have no religious affiliation; parents are making this choice because they are unsatisfied with public education. According to "Homeschool in America," a report issued by the National Center for Education Statistics in 2003, a whopping 75% of parents who homeschool indicated that they do so because they "believe they can give their child a better education" and wanted to take their children out of a "poor learning environment at school."

In 2010, there were over *2 million* students homeschooled. Some students choose to take online classes if they are available. In fact, there are a growing number of K-12 online schools with online companies such as K12 Inc (www.k12.com) taking the lead in providing online curriculum and schools like the Florida Virtual School (www.flvs.net) becoming a popular supplemental or even total alternative to the traditional public schools in the state of

Florida and beyond. Several other states (California, Arizona, Louisiana, Connecticut, etc.) also provide online K-12 schools for students—and the trend continues to grow. Online learning can provide opportunities for lessons to tap into the multiple intelligences of students and address the problem of the "one size fits all" structure of the current education system. Many parents pay tuition to private schools *in addition* to the tax money they are paying to the failing public schools. Clearly, some schools are failing badly enough that parents are aggressively seeking alternatives.

**How America measures up**
Even with all of the money the U.S. spends on education, we are currently ranked as "average" in comparison to other developed countries. In 2009, the Organization for Economic Co-operation and Development (OECD) reported that out of a score of 1000, America received an average of approximately only 500 in reading, math and science. These scores rank us 14th out of 34 OECD countries, 17th for science and 25th for math, despite the U.S. spending some of the highest amounts in the world on education. Some of the countries that spend the least on education such as Singapore and Finland have the best educational performance and better skills.

**Reform challenges**
While most of you reading this book know that a new model for our educational system is imperative, you also know that educational reform is easier and clearer in theory than in implementation. Many parties are involved, not just students. One challenge for reform includes labor agreements with some teachers unions that restrict certain changes.

Another is lack of infrastructure. A new curriculum would need to be developed, new measuring sticks would need to be set in place, and money would have to be reallocated from administration or other sources to technology tools for students and teachers. In fact, the very paradigm of "administration" may need to shift to new conceptions of how running a district or school would look in a digitally-converted learning environment.

Old ways of thinking also hinder reform. The current structure has become so widely accepted for so many years that it is difficult for stakeholders to think outside the box.

But we *must* make the shift if we ever want to actively encourage our young ones to take ownership of their studies. We have to think like them, find out what's important to them, and how they learn best. The good news is, our world is well-equipped for us to do just that.

## Importance of technology
The journey into the digital realm has worked exponentially well for businesses like banking, insurance and retail. Think of the countless hours saved by being able to pay a bill online or buy something from the comfort of your home rather than having to jump in the car and go to the store, find what you need in a 40,000 square-foot space, and then stand in a long line to pay.

The Internet has changed far more of how we live than most people even consider—because it's so commonplace now. Why should our education be any different?

Digital education is not using technology just for technology's sake. It is not taking textbooks and planting them in a digital sphere. Digital education offers us the ability to develop an ever-evolving curriculum that engages students and makes them accountable utilizing what we know about how students learn best in this day and age. It allows us to encourage the engagement of each student, providing each with a sense of ownership over his or her own education instead of something that's required—and connecting students to content that ignites thought and prompts questions that lead them to want to investigate further.

This model promotes proactive students, students who feel a sense of accomplishment rather than a sense of stupidity or inferiority. By placing technology into the hand of each student along with well-developed syllabi and by placing teachers in more of a facilitator's role, each student will be able to seek information about particular subjects for him- or herself. For one example of how this looks in practice, visit www.kidslikeblogs.org

Unfortunately, many schools are underutilizing digital space and sticking to teaching lessons in class and reading from textbooks. In some cases, the cost of textbooks is so high that schools can no longer afford them, so students must share. This is, indeed, an archaic approach in a world that abounds with so many resources readily available at our fingertips.

What's encouraging is that more and more students are taking online courses. In 2000, only 45,000 students took an online course. By 2009, this number had risen to more than 3 million. Imagine students being able to learn about a particular subject at their own pace, whether quickly or slowly, and being able to test what they're learning while they're learning it. Or imagine them having remote access to a great teacher who can ignite a passion in them. Or in the case of blended learning, students learn concepts and lessons online prior to class and then put what they learned into practice during precious class time.

Here is an example of this in practice. Upon visiting the Mooresville Graded School District (MGSD) in Mooresville, N.C., Jean Patton-Coble, instructional facilitator for the North Carolina Department of Public Instruction noted: "Imagine students blogging about predicting what will happen to Hamlet, building geometric models that can be manipulated in 3D, completing an online survey that the teacher uses to drive what is taught next, or creating high quality content cartoons to publish on the web. The above is just a glimpse of my visit to Mooresville High School."

Learn more about the MGSD's digital conversion: http://www5.mgsd.k12.nc.us/staffsites/digitalconversion/Digital_Conversion//MGSD_Digital_Conversion.html

## The most effective learning

We need to better understand how students learn most effectively, and to focus on videos, motion graphic diagrams, and games in addition to more the traditional "words on a page" approach. Some students learn best when content and concepts are presented in a *visual* format. Words often take time and energy for students to process, especially for those students who have learning challenges; visuals are tools they can understand in nanoseconds. Teachers now have access to printable materials, instructions for experiments, and more—so that hands-on learners can have a richer education.

For example, a study conducted by two researchers at the University of Michigan showed that people who received cartoon instructions were 24 percent more likely to read them than those who received text-only instructions. In addition, more than 45 percent of the people with the cartoon instructions answered all of the questions correctly on a test three days after reading the instructions, whereas only 6 percent of those did the same with the text-only instructions.

Also, online games like the visually-oriented MIND Research Institute's ST Math have shown positive jumps of up to 14 percent in math proficiency during a five-year pilot study. Online games such as these encourage engagement in a potentially difficult subject rather than reading about concepts in a textbook.

Digital learning can encourage students to learn concepts until they achieve self-actualization and mastery, which is easier to gauge via computer than written tests.

## Don't limit education to one teaching approach

Why not place the emphasis on the strength of each student rather than fitting them to a cookie-cutter mold? Why not implement teaching modules that encourage the reaching of goals to help students feel a sense of achievement and build self-esteem—rather than trying to make them memorize information so they can pass tests and to feel stupid if they don't?

By giving students the guidance and freedom to explore the digital realm, we are not limiting them to the strengths and weaknesses of one teacher per subject, but giving them access to the world in a rather literal sense.

## Why now is the right time

For the first time ever in the history of the human race we are in a position to provide student-centered, student-motivated education. We have a balance of economics, legislation, culture and technology that can provide the best educational system possible for the 21st century global marketplace in which we live.

Ten or 20 years ago, we didn't have the connectivity or the information. The technology wasn't within everyone's reach. Now, technology is everywhere. It's at home. It's in the workspace. It's in the palms of our hands and at the tips of our fingers. Students of the current generation are knowledgeable and comfortable using technology.

In addition, stakeholders are beginning to realize that our educational system is in need of reform. Visionaries are beginning to think of ways to improve schools. Now that technology has become so widely available and people are beginning to recognize the failures of our schools, the time for reform is ripe.

## It's not only education—it's an improved society

Educational reform not only leads to the improvement of the educational system but ultimately to the betterment of society and the wellbeing and health of people. For example, increasing understanding of scientific and economic principles can lead to higher yields and better prices for crops and cattle. It can also lead to the reduction of certain diseases. As the adage goes, knowledge is power. Nothing could be more true.

We needed education reform yesterday. We have already lost some generations. Unfortunately, it's been over 10 years since No Child Left Behind was initiated, and we're not moving forward. So much emphasis is placed on "teaching to the test" but not enough emphasis on students actually learning.

This kind of access and innovation in digital devices and Internet resources has never been possible before. But it is possible now, and we can and should do it. This is our time to change the course of history. Years from now—our generation could be remembered as the one that brought educational excellence to any student no matter where they were located nor what circumstances they faced.

We cannot afford *not* to try. We won't! With your help, leadership and belief—we will create a world where no child is held back from reaching his or her potential.

**For Your Consideration**

1. If you could add more options for alternative types of education, what would they be?

2. What challenges to educational reform are present within your sphere of influence? How can you overcome them?

3. List the ways in which the Internet has changed our lives.

4. List ways that you can use the Internet to improve education in your sphere of influence.

5. Think about the ways that you learn best. How could things have been done in your classroom to help you learn better?

No Child Held Back™

## NOTES

_____

_____

_____

_____

_____

_____

_____

_____

_____

_____

_____

_____

_____

_____

_____

_____

## For Your Exploration

1. Research the systems of education for the Greek and Roman Empires. What kind of people had access to education during this time? What subjects were covered under the Greek and Roman "curricula"?

2. Research current approaches to education reform. What are common messages and common recommendations? From your research, why is now a pivotal time to make lasting change?

No Child Held Back™

## NOTES

_____

_____

_____

_____

_____

_____

_____

_____

_____

_____

_____

_____

_____

_____

_____

_____

## Talking Points

1. For the first time ever in the history of the human race, we are in a position to provide student-centered, student-motivated education.

We have a balance of economics, legislation, culture and technology that can provide the best educational system possible for the conditions we are living in.

2. Change and education excellence are happening in many pockets around the country. Some charter schools as well as private and public schools are realizing this vision—we just need to care enough to learn more about it—or to simply try it.

There are a lot of successful schools and methods out there. There are really good examples of reform and the value technology can bring to the education process. We need to be brave and change the way things are done—because it is the right thing to do!

3. Our education system and the results it provides are a matter of national security. We are losing our leadership role in the world for innovation. We are approaching the point of no return where our society would start to crumble!

What is the American dream if not the promise of a good future if you work hard enough? In today's reality a student's zip code determines the quality of education that student will receive. In reality it is literally impossible for children who are born to poor families to cross the economic/social divide to actually be successful. Do we want the "American Dream" to become the "American Memory"? If we don't act now and revolutionize our education system– it will become just that!

No Child Held Back™

## NOTES

_____

_____

_____

_____

_____

_____

_____

_____

_____

_____

_____

_____

_____

_____

_____

_____

_____

_____

YOVEL BADASH

# *What*

**In the last** three chapters, we examined why there is a need for an approach to education reform that is based on leveraging the vast array of technological resources available in the 21st century.

The next key ingredient for initiating real reform is to understand what this reform really entails.

What is the right vision for our education system? And what is behind this No Child Held Back vision? What are the relevant pieces? What are its finer elements? What are its implications?

The next two chapters provide an answer for these questions.

YOVEL BADASH

# 4
# THE NO CHILD HELD BACK APPROACH

**The first thing** to recognize about No Child Held Back is that it is indeed *an approach, a new vision*—a *way of thinking* and a *set of guidelines* for making key decisions about how schools engage students, technology and the communities around them. So what exactly would this approach look like, and what would it mean?

One of the first steps to changing something is realizing what works and what doesn't—and then taking a step back to reevaluate how to make improvements in the most effective manner. NCLB doesn't work. So, let's take a step back and see why.

From my previous chapters, you're already familiar with the premise behind NCHB, but what does it *really* look like, and what would it mean? To answer that, let's take a look at how it differs from No Child Left Behind.

NCHB takes the focus off from punishing schools for their perceived failures. Instead, it focuses on inspiring students to reach their full potential. Shouldn't education be focused on the students?

## Reigniting a love of learning and a sense of self-efficacy
Under NCLB, students become so worried about their standardized test scores that they become unable to truly learn. Students that are made to feel "dumb" or "inferior" by test scores

—stop trying. Now, to make these stagnant students be successful, states lower their standards.

Instead of making a test the measure of a student's success, NCHB celebrates the small victories on the journey to a good education.

| NCLB | NCHB |
|---|---|
| Uses fear and punishment methods to achieve program goals. | Encourages inspiration, ambition and self-actualization of students. |
| Utilizes periodic tests to measure comprehension with no remedy for poor performance in place except promoting the fear of failure. | Positive reinforcement through many small wins while pursuing a larger goal. |
| Lower state standards so they can be reached by all students. | Healthy competition, which helps students push themselves harder. |
| Predominantly uses traditional lecture and test without taking into account the way each student learns best. | Utilizes multiple learning modalities such as visual, tacticle, and auditory learning depending on individual students. |
| Teachers are under pressure to meet requirements, they are stressed, burdened with demands and the focus is off teaching. | Teachers are free and able to professionally develop; their focus is on inspiring their students. |
| Commonly places teachers in a subject area unrelated to their area of expertise so they lack any deep understanding. | Utilizes the full knowledge base of each teacher, who can then provide outstanding instruction. |
| Teaching to the test for fear the school will not receive federal funding. | Student-centered learning and curricula helps all students reach their maximum potential. |
| Teachers tend to be too distant from students because they have a full class to manage and teach lesson plans during class time. | Encourages the evolution of the teacher role to include more personal, one-on-one interactions with each student and adjusting the curricula as needed every step of the way. |
| The primary responsibility is on the school, placing the authority in the hands of the teachers and administrators and placing students in a passive role. | Encourages students to become engaged participants in their education and parents to take more responsibility in keeping their children on course. |
| Testing is used to determine what kind of funding schools receive and to measure Adequate Yearly Progress (which is hard to measure). | Testing is used as an actionable benchmark in order to adjust the curricula for each student if needed. |
| Teachers don't have the effective solutions they need—just evaluation and measurement systems. They are focused on testing and assessment. | Teachers have access to tools, content and support systems that make them more effective. Emphasis is on being the best teacher they can be. |

When students feel fulfilled by reaching small goals, they are more confident in tackling larger ones.

NCHB creates more engaged students by not allowing them to sit passively in their seats like sponges. They are given the reins to their own educational journey, and their success or lack thereof is based upon themselves.

## Giving teachers the power to innovate and inspire

NCLB specifies what to teach and when to teach it, often leading teachers to feel forced to move through material whether or not they see that students have mastered important skills. With its focus on open source education as a powerful tool for educating, NCHB encourages teachers to design and present content in visual, auditory, and tactile ways so that students of all learning styles will have a chance to internalize what is being taught. It also gives teachers the tools to help students discover what they are naturally drawn to, allowing them to pace their own learning, so that they can build on their strengths and experience school as a fun, joyful, and engaging place where they can truly shine.

## Retaining the best and brightest

Staggering statistics across the nation reveal that teachers leave in droves early in their careers. According to *"Teacher Retention: A Critical National Problem"*, a report issued by the Haberman Foundation in 2008, 50% of teachers leave the profession in their first five years. In schools with a population of 75% or more minority, low income, or Hispanic—the teacher turnover rate exceeded 20% in 2007 alone. The emotional and developmental cost to students is, in and of itself, cause for alarm. Over and over again, correlations have been made between the least effective schools and lack of a strong body of teachers. Add to this the monetary costs and the imperative for a new approach becomes non-negotiable. The Haberman Foundation report cited that under the current resignation trends, a district that lost 30% of its teachers between 1998 and 2001—just three years—may spend $30 to $40 million to replace the talent.

To ensure that content is delivered in the best way and ensure that teachers are set up to win for the long-haul, NCHB emphasizes both selecting the best teachers and providing the most useful, applicable professional development to them. It focuses on making existing teachers more effective!

In a recent study, McKinsey looked at what is different about top school systems to understand how they enable better teaching and enhance learning.

The research team concluded, "Three things matter most:
1) Getting the right people to become teachers,
2) Developing them into effective instructors, and
3) Ensuring that the system is able to deliver the best possible instruction for every child."

The McKinsey study went on to explain that the countries with the top-performing systems in the world – Singapore, Finland, and South Korea – focus on recruiting, developing, and retaining 100 percent of top graduates from education programs. In fact, it is their nations' top priority. In contrast, only 23 percent of new teachers in the U.S. come from the top third of their classes and just 14 percent from high poverty schools.

Pursuing the top third will increase the quality of teachers in our schools and push all students in education programs to try harder and become better. Doesn't it make sense that our teachers should be the best and brightest, igniting students along the way, serving as leaders for the next generation? Wouldn't it be ideal that teachers in our country were held in as high esteem as doctors?

Think about it. Doctors go through 8 years of higher education and are required to participate in professional development opportunities so that they will not cause harm to a person's body. But teachers are only required to have four years of higher education and may or may not be required to participate in professional learning.

If they do participate in professional development, often the training takes place in the nooks and crannies of days, months, and years where teachers are already overwhelmed with too much paperwork than they can feasibly handle. Yet they are responsible for protecting and developing the minds of students who may one day become those doctors.

Why are teachers not considered to be as influential? Shouldn't they have the tools they need to do their jobs properly? Why won't we help our teachers become more effective?

Because teachers are entrusted with shaping the minds of students and changing the world, only the best candidates should be selected. For example, in Finland, teachers must hold a master's degree, complete 35 weeks of study in the subject they are to teach, and have 60 credits of pedagogical study. Furthermore, they must have an excellent command of their native language.

How much would education improve in the U.S. if the hiring process were more selective for teachers? What if our best and brightest students would want to become teachers? How would it impact each child's life if teachers were set up to win with robust professional development?

It is time we realize that teachers are among the most important members of our society because they influence society on such a large scale. This can't happen overnight and would require a fundamental change in our culture and perception of education.

Under NCLB, teachers become so pressured to bring their students up to a "standard" that they focus all their attention on teaching only subjects that will be tested. Then they have no time to help students that need more instruction, and certainly no time to challenge students who want to learn more.

NCHB changes the role of a teacher. He or she becomes an educational guide who adjusts the curriculum for each student as needed and helps them set goals for their own learning.

With changing roles and changing students comes a need for ongoing training and development. Using open source technology as a platform, NCHB provides teachers with the kind of fluid, flexible professional development that allows them to choose what they most need.

Other reform initiatives have proven the impact of a well-equipped, empowered teacher. For example, Teach for America recruits the most promising future leaders of America and places them for two years or more in low-income communities as a means of eliminating educational inequality. The result? A number of studies have shown that these teachers have a stronger impact on students than some teachers who came from more conventional teaching routes. A large part of NCHB's purpose is to develop and retain teachers just like Teach for America turns out—those who are able to roll with the punches, learn new skills and think creatively where needed while engaging students.

NCHB also seeks to use technology to connect teachers to each other, whether they are teaching in South Africa, Canada, the UK, Brazil, or the U.S.. NCHB's use of online technology assists teachers in becoming more effective. Human beings are, by nature, social creatures. We thrive on connection and the sharing of ideas. There are already some outstanding teachers in the current system, but how can we get them to connect with others? One example is the Bill & Melinda Gates Foundation, a leader for the improvement of education in America. Among their many initiatives, they recently launched a $3.5 million multi-platform service that delivers professional development videos to teachers over the Internet, public television, cable and other digital outlets. To date, more than 13,500 teachers and educators have joined the community to share ideas, lesson plans and teaching methods.

Most teachers choose this profession because they want to make a difference. The NCHB approach gives them the resources and power to do just that.

Empowered teachers are able to fulfill their dreams of making a marked impact, strongly increasing the likelihood that they will remain in and thrive in their careers for the long haul.

**Testing as a learning tool**
Under NCHB, testing is not used as a way to determine if a school should receive funding. Testing becomes an indicator of mastery or competence in an area. It shows where small adjustments need to be made for each student so that they can then achieve more. A student's worth is not based upon a test score. The test scores simply defines what assistance a student needs to actualize his or her full capability.

As you can see, NCHB moves the current educational system from a fear-based, test-centric, low standard and mediocre approach to an approach that is student-centered, grounded in personalized education from outstanding teachers.

Some may say that NCHB is impossible; that it can't be done. Well, imagine trying to implement any sort of educational success in one of the roughest areas of America: Harlem. Geoffrey Canada, who was featured in the documentary *Waiting for Superman*, decided to take on his neighborhood and turn it around despite the poverty, crime, and violence taking place. He was a catalyst in moving the Harlem Children's Zone forward with the intention to help both children and families in an effort to break the cycle of generational poverty. The focus is "cradle to college," which means that children start in the program as early in their lives as possible and that they have a group of supportive adults around them who understand how to make them succeed. Since its inception in the 70s, the program now covers more than 100 city blocks of Harlem and serves thousands of students and families in the area with not only educational but social, community and health services as well. His program has been so successful, in fact, that the Obama Administration is applying it to over 20 in-need neighborhoods throughout the US through the Promise Neighborhoods program.

Through his program, Canada has proven that improvements can be made anywhere. His program also shows the absolute need for parental involvement. Children need leadership, and they'll find it somewhere, whether that's at home with a strong parent or on the streets.

Another successful leader in this area has been Michelle Rhee. Her past work includes serving as Chancellor of the Washington, D.C., public school district and founder of The New Teacher Project, which helps to train teachers to become better instructors in the classroom. Most recently, Rhee founded StudentsFirst as a grassroots movement to change the protection of teacher seniority. In most states, it is difficult to fire tenured teachers no matter their performance. Rhee's vision is to elevate teaching through performance-based evaluations of teachers, encouraging parental involvement, and giving all students access to great schools.

### Power of community and cross-cultural collaboration
No one company or person can do everything. But we are creating and maintaining a framework approach that is flexible and useful enough to fit everyone anywhere and everywhere in the world.

That's why the No Child Held Back approach incorporates a powerful consortium where parents, teachers, school administrators, learning experts, citizens, business leaders, education publishers, and technology providers can work together to make student-centered NCHB happen.

NCHB can work as much in New York City as it can in rural Africa. Why? Because it's student-centered and flexible. Each school is different, each community is different, and definitely, each student is different. The NCHB approach takes all of this into consideration and respects these differences. With focus on the abilities of each student, highly effective teachers, and easy access to multiple digital tools, the NCHB concept transcends cultural, ethnic, geographic, financial, and socioeconomic lines. Through the planning of educational thought leaders and those passionate to see reform, NCHB can become a reality.

In fact, the NCHB framework could be implemented *even while conforming to NCLB mandated performance levels.* Even just changing the focus from generic education to more individually-focused education based on each student's academic and vocational aspirations would result in happier, more interested students. It is time that we rethink what our students need to learn and what they would like to learn. Then we must find the most effective ways to deliver that knowledge to them.

Now is the time for all stakeholders to become involved. You can be the catalyst to inspire not only a school, but an entire world where children and communities thrive. By adding your unique voice to the choir of visionaries who are already making the No Child Held Back approach a reality, you can leave a legacy that will have a marked impact.

As you have seen so far, the stakes are too high not to take action and add your voice. With rapid pace global change as the norm, we simply can't afford to hold back one more generation of students, nor can we afford to let our teachers, our greatest national resource, fall into resignation and malaise. The costs—emotional and financial—are just too high. We must give those on the front lines the tools they need to be successful. This can happen as we all bring our ideas, perspectives, and thoughts together in a powerful community.

The next chapter of this book moves from the bird's eye view of NCHB laid out here and narrows in on concrete, key elements. The second half of the book offers concrete tools that you can use to begin implementing change now. Devour what's there, enjoy, and let your fellow partners in educational transformation know what you are doing. Join the conversation and lend your voice at: www.nochildheldback.com.

## For Your Consideration

1. What are the three differences between NCLB and NCHB that you feel are the most important for you to embrace right now? How will you take action?

2. How do you feel about teachers being protected based upon seniority rather than effectiveness?

3. What requirements should the U.S. use to select teachers? How much do you think teachers should be paid?

4. How much professional development should be required for teachers? What can you do to help teachers within your sphere of influence become better equipped for their jobs?

No Child Held Back™

## NOTES

**For Your Exploration**

1. Go to www.hcz.org. Which of the programs do you find most inspiring?   Is there a similar way that you can influence your community?

2. Go to www.studentsfirst.org. Is your state a participant? Have you taken action to help improve education in your area? Explore the website to learn what you can do.

3. Have a reform topic you want to add your voice to, or get insight on from others? Go to www.nochildheldback.com, complete your free membership to join the consortium, and initiate a powerful dialogue.

No Child Held Back

## NOTES

_____

_____

_____

_____

_____

_____

_____

_____

_____

_____

_____

_____

_____

_____

_____

_____

_____

## Talking Points

1. The NCHB approach is a systematic view of education that allow for inspired teaching, tangible community engagement with schools, and customization of learning content and learning paths to meet the varied needs of individual learners.

Under this approach, every educational stakeholder can thrive.

*Parents* thrive because they have access to resources that they can use to support their children at home and because they have immediate access to what is happening in the life of their child's school.

*Teachers* thrive because they have the resources to meet the needs of every child in their classroom, and no longer have to worry about whether or not they have enough textbooks or enough computer stations. They also thrive with access to ongoing sustained professional development helping them to be the best they can be.

*Students* thrive because they have access to information that gives them the opportunity to learn content from different perspectives; within that, they can find a perspective that speaks to them. They also thrive because learning is hands-on and in real time; they have immediate feedback for their participation and engagement. Finally, they thrive because the approach to learning is a match for how they process and use information.

*Business and community stakeholders* thrive because they have real-time access to the needs of a school, and easy ways to collaborate with school officials to set up community-school partnerships.

2. NCHB is an approach that can work for any school district, anywhere around the globe, leveling the playing field to ensure that every child on the planet has access to a high quality education.

Because the NCHB approach is rooted in technology, students in Africa have access to stellar teachers in the U.S. and vice versa. A classroom in Nevada studying, say, the fall of the Berlin Wall and the impact of World War II on post-war Germany can have access to post-war scholars who have first-hand experience living through that transition.

The limits to what is possible through digital education are truly only bound by one's imagination.

No Child Held Back

**NOTES**

_____

_____

_____

_____

_____

_____

_____

_____

_____

_____

_____

YOVEL BADASH

# 5
# KEY ELEMENTS OF NO CHILD HELD BACK

**The NCHB approach** holds a set of key elements. Here we will elaborate on each one and introduce research and background information to support our position.

It is important that you really "get" the value of each element and its importance in the overall scheme of No Child Held Back. Individually-paced learning, support for all learning types and multiple intelligences, world-class content, classwork and homework transformation, connecting schools to the local community, as well as customer satisfaction assessment are all vital in moving a school system from a factory approach to a student-centered, customized learning program. What methodologies and tools change when the paradigm shifts from No Child Left Behind to No Child Held Back?

**Encouragement Mindset.** No Child Left Behind emphasizes failure, punishment and meeting minimal achievement standards. No Child Held Back is focused on inspiration, ambition, learning and self-actualization for both students and teachers. It invites levels of emotional and intellectual engagement only achieved through intrinsic rewards, not external punishments.

**Positive Reinforcement.** Teachers note that students today have shorter attention spans than previous generations. Keeping students motivated and on-task during study time is increasingly difficult in an "always on" world. Parents and children are bombarded with hundreds of TV channels, billions of web pages, social media interactions, mobile communication, and thousands of daily distractions. Never has consistent positive reinforcement been more important to learning. Providing students with multiple opportunities to earn many small wins as they master new course skills while pursuing the larger goal of course mastery is crucial for boosting the attention, motivation and inspiration required for high achievement.

**Healthy Competitiveness.** When students know that nothing will hold them back and they can see peers rewarded for reaching personal achievement goals, they will be more inclined to push themselves forward in a healthy, competitive way. Charter schools have clearly shown how positive peer pressure successfully encourages students and creates role models among disadvantaged students who have few other positive role models outside the classroom. Allowing dedicated students to enjoy special activities and rewards is a great motivator for encouraging their peers to try harder to attain their own rewards.

**Multiple Learning Modalities.** In order for all students to excel, it is important to support multiple learning modalities. Teachers need to make sure they have ways to help each student learn as fast and as thoroughly as possible. Some students learn best by reading, some by listening to lectures, and others through active participation in projects. Giving students the flexibility to choose their optimal learning modes teaches them to take greater personal responsibility for their learning and helps keep them engaged with the learning process.

**Outstanding Teachers.** The impact of an individual teacher is much greater than the impact of a school environment. "Your child is actually better off in a 'bad' school with an excellent teacher than in an excellent school with a bad teacher," Malcolm Gladwell wrote in a recent article for The *New Yorker*. He cited a report by Stanford economist Eric Hanushek that explains how "students of a very bad teacher will learn, on average, half a year's worth of material in one school year. The students in the class of a very good teacher will learn a year-and-a-half's worth of material. That difference amounts to a year's worth of learning in a single year." According to Hanushek, one would have to reduce class size by 50 percent to achieve a similar learning improvement. He asserts that simply replacing the worst 6 to 10 percent of teachers with merely average teachers could close the U.S. performance gap with high performing nations.

This could also be achieved by providing these "bad" teachers with the tools, incentives, and motivation to improve, excel and become more effective. In their study of the world's best school systems, McKinsey & Company also emphasizes the importance of teacher quality. The report explains, "Teachers need to be able to assess precisely the strengths and weaknesses of each individual student they teach, select the appropriate instructional methods to help them learn, and deliver instruction in an effective and efficient manner." Building a cadre of outstanding teachers in a school system requires success in two areas: 1) recruiting high quality expert teachers with talent and drive, and 2) making a commitment to ongoing professional development and coaching to continuously enhance the skills of existing teachers.

This is why the No Child Held Back framework must extend to teachers as well. No teacher should be held back in the quest to become the most skilled educator he or she can become. The work of teaching must engage each teacher's best skills and talents to provide satisfying, challenging work. Compensation and incentives must be aligned to reward excellent performance and increase retention among high performers.

**Outstanding Instruction.** No matter how skilled teachers may be in preparing lesson plans, designing tests, or managing a classroom, their students' achievement will be severely limited if they lack strong instructional ability. While a few teachers are simply poor instructors, a much more common problem with instructional quality is a teacher's lack of subject-matter expertise. The common practice of assigning teachers to classes unrelated to their academic majors, minors, or teaching certification training is at fault.

Teacher qualification expert Richard M. Ingersoll recently analyzed data from more than 5,000 school districts, 11,000 schools, and 53,000 teachers to assess the pervasiveness of out-of-field teaching. He found that, overall, 38 percent of all math teachers in grades 7-12 lack a major or minor in math, math education, or related disciplines like engineering, statistics, or science. About one-third of English teachers lack a related degree. Similarly, 28 percent of science teachers and 25 percent of social studies teachers lack backgrounds in their subjects. This problem of under-qualified teachers is especially rampant in disadvantaged schools where poverty is high and recruiting quality teachers is difficult.

Without a deep understanding of their subject matter, how can teachers be expected to deliver outstanding instruction to every student every day? In the No Child Held Back approach, teachers and administrators must make sure that all children have access to the outstanding instruction needed to reach their highest potential.

**Student-Centered Learning.** Helping students reach their potential requires finding ways to support a variety of learning methods, abilities, and speeds. Personalized, student-centered curricula allow teachers to help all students reach their maximum potential. Slower students must be allowed to move at their own pace and master each required concept before moving on to the next step; advanced students must be challenged to enhance their grasp of basic concepts with engaging, supplemental knowledge and more complex work. When students have difficulty with a concept, teachers need flexible ways to help students attain mastery by utilizing custom remedial assignments or alternate methods of presenting material.

Also vital to student-centered learning is course variety. Each student has unique educational and vocational goals. Allowing students to include courses that directly relate to their personal interests and aspirations is a powerful motivator for keeping them engaged in school and the learning process. If a student wants to learn Chinese, take chess as an elective, or add vocational courses to prepare for a non-college career, depriving them of those learning opportunities is holding them back. Luckily, new technology innovations make it easier than ever for schools and districts to broaden their course offerings through traditional, blended, and virtual learning opportunities.

**Teacher Role Evolution.** No Child Held Back dramatically changes the teacher's role in student learning. To be successful, teachers must have more personal, one-on-one interactions with each student and assess each student individually. Studies show that these highly personal interactions yield significant increases in learning outcomes. In 1984, a research group led by educational psychologist Benjamin Bloom found "that students given one-on-one attention reliably perform two standard deviations better than their peers who stay in a regular classroom." This is the difference between median performance and advancing to the 98th percentile.

Within the No Child Held Back framework, the teacher's role is to inspire and lead, to develop character, and to help fulfill each student's potential. Teachers customize the path for each student and make sure each student not only meets minimal requirements, but exceeds those requirements to reach their full potential. This becomes a much more satisfying role for individuals who enter teaching with aspirations of helping guide future generations.

**Student and Parent Responsibility.** Because of the individualized, student-centered nature of NCHB, the balance of responsibility for learning shifts dramatically. Students and parents enjoy greater empowerment, but also bear a much greater responsibility for managing the student's academic growth. Students must be trained to be proactive in seeking the instruction and guidance they need. Parents need greater transparency into their children's academic performance and actionable tools to help their children learn. If a child falls behind in a subject, it is important for the teacher to be able to enlist the help of the parent in administering remedial learning programs to get the child back on track, regardless of the parent's own level of education. Providing parents with effective tools and guidance makes it easier and more likely that they will be able to encourage and assist their children.

**Community Partnership.** Unfortunately, some parents are unable or unwilling to assume the responsibility of helping their children succeed academically. Domestic situations such as substance abuse, poverty, parental illiteracy, language challenges, and absentee parenting due to divorce, incarceration, or demanding work schedules can severely impact parental involvement. This is one reason why the NCHB framework encourages a strong emphasis on both community outreach and technology adoption. Find out how your school can reach out to its community and increase its technology use, or share ways you get your community involved, visit: www.nochildheldback.com

The more a school engages with its community, the more resources and support systems become available to students. Building strong connections with volunteers, community literacy and tutoring groups, social service organizations and even government programs can help fill in some of the gaps left by unfavorable family environments.

Technology can play a vital role in connecting community education stakeholders, as well as providing teachers, guidance personnel and administrators with easier, more effective ways of finding the supplemental help their students need.

**Testing as an Actionable Benchmark.** In the student-centered model, standardized test results move beyond a punitive requirement for schools to become actionable information for teachers who can then use the results to design customized remedial programs to help lagging students catch up with their peers. The actual purpose and usage of testing changes from measuring each student against the group to that of a tool for helping support each student's individualized academic growth. Teachers can evaluate the scores of incoming students to customize each one's learning programs for the upcoming year. They can use the annual results as benchmarks to evaluate the relative success of their learning programs and adjust as needed. Educators may find new approaches to testing helpful.

Testing under the NCHB approach will support the assessment of each student's optimum learning modalities and how teachers can help craft more effective assignments. Traditional quizzes and tests can be used in new ways to encourage students to learn. When students pass the test they move to the next unit of study with their peers. Students scoring below the norm receive customized remedial work before moving forward.

As you can see, NCHB is dedicated to making education centered upon the student. This is done through transforming emphasis of punishing schools that do not have a critical mass of students pass a test to an emphasis on truly educating the individual student. When the students begin achieving small goals, they receive rewards and encouragement. It is also done by ensuring that teachers become their best, able to select and deliver the best content. Finally, it is done through ensuring that each student is helped to achieve his/her maximum potential.

NCHB emphasizes the use of technology within the classroom and at home to make the best learning experiences available to each individual student. In addition, students and parents are encouraged to take ownership of their own education process. And teachers receive the training and tools that they need to be successful.

Are you on board with this vision? Join us and lend your voice to it! If you would like learn how you can help and partner with educational visionaries around the world or in your area, visit www.nochildheldback.com

## For Your Consideration

1. What elements of NCHB resonate for your particular situation? List the areas in which your local school is excelling and the areas in which it can improve.

2. What are some rewards that can be used to promote healthy competition? What are some ways to keep all students encouraged?

3. Think of a subject to be taught. Now name three different ways that the same information can be presented for different learning styles.

4. Discuss some ways that the effectiveness of a teacher can be assessed.

5. Name some professional development opportunities that should be available to teachers and school administrators.

6. Think about when you were in school. What subjects did you want to study but did not have the opportunity to study?

7. What are some ways that parents and students can both take more responsibility? Think of educational opportunities that can be offered to parents.

No Child Held Back

## NOTES

_____

_____

_____

_____

_____

_____

_____

_____

_____

_____

_____

_____

_____

_____

_____

## For Your Exploration

1. Do an Internet search for "multiple intelligences". How does this philosophy apply to the current school system? How does it apply to NCHB?

2. Do an Internet search for "learning styles". What is *your* learning style? How can you use this information to improve how you learn?

No Child Held Back
™

## NOTES

_____

_____

_____

_____

_____

_____

_____

_____

_____

_____

_____

_____

_____

_____

_____

_____

## Talking Points

1. NCHB incorporates an encouragement mindset, positive reinforcement, healthy competitiveness, multiple learning modalities, outstanding teachers, teacher role evolution, outstanding instruction, student-centered learning, testing as an actionable benchmark, student responsibility, parent responsibility, and community partnerships.

All of these elements work together as a *system* that leads to students accessing and capitalizing on their unique talents and gifts, leading them to excel in school and in life.

Just as a puzzle is not complete without one of its pieces, the NCHB approach will not have its intended impact unless all elements have been carefully thought through and put in place within schools and school districts across the world.

Or, just like the human body, if one system (i.e. circulatory, muscular, neurological) is not functioning well, all the others suffer in some way.

No Child Held Back

## NOTES

_____

_____

_____

_____

_____

_____

_____

_____

_____

_____

_____

_____

_____

_____

_____

_____

YOVEL BADASH

# *How*

**So far, we** have explored why education reform is critical today and what it looks like from the NCHB standpoint.

The final ingredient key to initiating reform is having a set of mechanisms for implementing the reform—in other words, *knowing how* to get it done.

In the remaining chapters of this book, you will be introduced to a set of tools and resources that will allow you to get started turning the NCHB vision into a reality in your own educational community.

YOVEL BADASH

# 6
# PERSONALIZED LEARNING TOOLS

**Personalized learning tools** pre-2000 might have meant a scientific calculator, a compass, a pencil and a good eraser. However, the importance of personalized learning tools in the last decade has taken on an entirely new meaning, radically shifting the way education takes place. It is critical for each student to be able to learn on their own and at their own pace. Also critical is the need to teach the same body of knowledge in different ways in order to fit different intelligence types. The good news is that there are literally hundreds of new tools out there just waiting for students to use.

In the last five years alone, as technologies have matured and educators and "edupreneurs" (education entrepreneurs) have begun to better grasp what works and what goes viral, there has been an explosion in learning tools for students in both K-12 and higher education. Technological (bandwidth, devices), cultural (tech-native students), and economic factors (budget-strapped schools homed in by innovative edtech startups) have converged to yield the current scene.

Internet and social media have exploded onto this scene at rates that far exceed any previous mass communication platforms. According to social media pundit Erik Qualman, radio took 38 years to reach 50 million users; television took 13, the Internet just 4, the iPod only 3 years, and Facebook added 100 million users in just 9 months. Connecting online is natural to the latest generation of the population. For example, 96 percent of so-called "Gen Y" members are part of a social network.

The use of digital education is proving to be a good thing. According to the U.S. Department of Education, online students outperform traditional students with 1 in 6 higher education students taking an online course. Pew Research says 57 percent of experts think that a tech-fueled learning paradigm will be determined by student choice. In the next decade, most students will be in a blended environment; that is, they will be learning partly online in groups according to interest, mastery and skill. Tech spending isn't about to get cut, either; in 2008 it was $47.6 billion, and forecasts say $93 billion by 2018.

While our theme is all about *personalized learning tools*, it's important to know that a wider concept is at work here. Notably, some of the following terms and phrases are complete educational movements in and of themselves; others are buzzwords or even clichés adopted to describe a goal or intention of educators in pursuit of learning excellence. But whatever the label, you can find them all in the same bucket of *personalized learning*. Education is rapidly moving to:

Individualized instruction
Customized learning
Personalized learning
Adaptive learning
Intelligent adaptive learning
Differentiated instruction
Personal digital learning
Student 'playlists'
Learner profiles
Individual learning programs
Select a project > acquire a mentor > demonstrate mastery - learning
Project-based learning
Authentic learning
Student-centered learning
Personalized learning environments (PLEs)
Social media in education

*Individualized instruction* for personalized learning bases content, instructional technology and the pace of learning on the abilities and interests of the student. This is in contrast with *mass instruction*, where the modus operandi has been "everything's the same for all, round 'em up, and move 'em out." Personalized learning tailors pedagogy, curriculum and the learning environment to meet the needs of the learner—with technology playing a large part.

Personalized learning allows for an education that's tailor fit. Gardner's theory of multiple intelligences grants importance to individuals as they approach learning in their own varied ways, rather than a mentality that shoves students unnaturally into the mass instruction model at the expense of our future leaders, artists and engineers.

While personalization differs from differentiation as it introduces more student choice (anytime, anywhere learning), there are yet targets to be met. Nonetheless, learners have an opportunity to learn in their own way and time, according to their learning style and intelligences.

Technology is a powerful tool, providing research, communication, collaboration, discourse, and a record of it all that can then be pushed back to work for a learner, which leads us to the notion of *adaptive* learning.

Knewton, the test prep company, is a prime example of a company with a product applying this; but there are more. Others are joining this trend as data systems get smarter at instantaneously considering a student's strengths, weaknesses and overall learning style.

While Knewton initially made its footprint via the test prep market, college readiness and test prep are but a couple of ways they tackle the broader education picture—which actually includes adaptive learning, flipped classrooms, blended learning, digital education and STEM education. For example, they use a cloud-based platform for adaptive learning with concept-level data to create uniquely personalized learning plans, allowing educators to tailor their content to the exact needs of individual students.

Content providers use Knewton to transform student experiences into personalized learning experiences through an intelligent infrastructure that underlies the student's learning path, creating a unique individual user experience. A personalized learning environment suddenly takes on more meaning through such adaptive learning technologies. Digital or electronic portfolios begin to blur with embedded assessments.

With this move toward using technology content providers as an alternative to textbooks and the like, it's important to note that too much automation will take us backward to the old model, not forward. The technology needs to serve the teacher and the students, not the other way around. Far too often, in today's world, under the current paradigm, teachers are serving the technology. They have to take time to learn the system or program they are using, and follow *its* rules of order.

What's possible in an NCHB model is an open platform where teachers can use multiple tools to create and invent what they most need for the students they have in the moment.

NaMaYa, Inc. is an example of a company providing a technology platform in which teachers can pick and choose resources that work best for them, as well as access user-friendly tools that allow them to create content and easily plug it in to a framework custom-designed for their school and/or district.

With a fluid approach to technological content—real-time feedback, student profiles and "Netflix-style" smart-recommendation 'playlists' generate a new approach to learning—one quite a bit more fascinating to the learner, who can now be directly catered to, attended to and truly helped—without having to wait for a teacher to make his/her rounds with dozens of other students vying for attention.

Please understand that NCHB does *not* embrace the idea of placing a student in front of a computer for 8 hours a day while the teacher does nothing. However, using technology can free a teacher to develop other hands-on learning activities, customize learning paths for students, and offer assistance when it is needed.

For example, NaMaYa PD, a teacher professional development provider, offers a cloud-based platform in which schools are able to individualize PD curricula, provide personalized professional development for staff, access content from other sources, promote teacher online social learning, connect the teacher community, create original content and more. Think of how much can be accomplished when the walls of the school are knocked down and geographic boundaries are overcome through technology.

**Statistics**
According to the BLE Group, a consultancy of 100 active, tech-savvy superintendents from around the country, more than 50 percent of students entering high school are two or more years behind in at least one subject on meeting the academic grade-level standards. Further, less than 40 percent are proficient, and only 5 percent are advanced. What do we do about the *more than 50 percent of students* who are missing the necessary prerequisite skills to master their current standards?

More educators are asking themselves that same question, and the solution providers in the education marketplace are beginning to respond with some real options.

One great place to learn about the latest technology is at the annual Florida Education Technology Conference (FETC), one of the largest U.S. education technology conferences. There you will find nearly 400 companies exhibiting innovative tools. Educational leaders and technology experts exchange techniques and strategies for teaching and learning success. Those in attendance include teachers, principals, deans, district administrators, curriculum designers, media specialists, technology directors and others in and around education. Interestingly, many presenters support personalized e-learning in K-12 education.

Currently, some of the best options for personalized learning include subtle shifts in thinking and using tools already at the disposal of many students. With mobile portfolio applications and continuing expansion of mobile devices for academic use, personalized learning further continues as a watchword in education.

## Smart call

Research shows that smartphones may lead to added study time for students. Students with access to educational materials via smartphones study about 40 minutes longer each week, according to a new report by the mobile study tool provider StudyBlue. Researchers who looked at data from nearly 1 million students who use the site found that they use their smartphones to study while at school or at work, during commutes, while exercising and at other times. It's education on the go. The research didn't link the additional study time with improved grades but did show that students with smartphones also were more likely to track assignments and grades. Personalized learning solutions are literally all around us—and in our students' hands.

## Moving forward online

A further look into research on technology and learning reveals certain key trends as highlighted in the 2010 Speak Up report from the massive (over 300,000 students responded) online survey group Project Tomorrow:

• The number of high school students who are taking online classes for school credit has almost doubled since Speak Up 2008.
• The number of teachers who have taught online classes has tripled since Speak Up 2008. However, we still have more work to do to help teachers learn how to effectively leverage online learning to drive student achievement and increase their own productivity.
• Even as aspiring teachers are gaining experience with online classes and online professional learning communities as part of their teacher preparation programs, only 4 percent report that they are learning how to teach online classes in their instructional methods courses.
• Administrators are beginning to shift their focus of online learning from only professional development for teachers to also include online classes for students.
• Thirty-three percent of parents report they have taken an online class for their own professional needs or personal interests. Parents' personal experiences with online learning are affecting how their children view the benefits of online learning as well.

*Source: http://www.tomorrow.org/speakup/ learning21Report_2010_Update.html*

## Shift in perspective

*The New 3 E's of Education: Enabled, Engaged, Empowered: How Today's Educators are Advancing a New Vision for Teaching and Learning* is an excellent resource for teachers who are undergoing a digital conversion. All three of the "3 E's" converging at the same time has opened up a new window of possibility for achieving the promise of technology to transform education. Evidence of this shift in perspective and vision by educators is noted in some comparative Speak Up findings over the past few years:

• Over twice as many teachers and administrators have a personal smartphone today than in 2008.
• While only 11 percent of teachers regularly updated their social networking site in 2007, over 44 percent are active Facebook users in 2010. Forty-five percent of administrators are also Facebook users now.
• Reflecting the exploding interest in digital content and e-textbooks, four times more administrators (35 percent) are concerned today about how to evaluate the quality of digital resources than just one year ago (9 percent).
• Thirty percent of teachers are now using podcasts and videos in their classroom instruction – an increase of over 50 percent since 2008.
• Teacher interest in teaching an online class has grown by 76 percent in just two years.
• And as classroom instruction is becoming more digitally-based, administrators are ranking digital equity and student home technology access as a much bigger issue.

While only 12 percent of administrators listed digital equity as a concern in 2007, 30 percent of our education leaders today consider student access an important district challenge.

*Source: http://www.tomorrow.org/speakup/pdfs/ SU10_3EofEducation_Educators.pdf*

## Inside today's classroom

To best understand this new vision for engaging, enabling and empowering learning through technology, it's vital to see realities of tech use in the classroom. Teachers and administrators both report using all kinds of technology for their jobs; their usage closely mirrors students' own vision for socially-based, untethered and digitally-rich learning—but of course to a much lesser degree of frequency or depth.

Nearly all teachers (96 percent) and administrators (99 percent) are tapping into communications tools to connect with peers or parents; though a far lesser amount of teachers (36 percent) are using these same tools to connect with their students.

Educators are regularly using the Internet for research (almost 90 percent) and reading text-based resources (61 percent) including blogs and wikis (33 percent). Slightly more administrators (68 percent) than teachers (53 percent) are creating multi-media presentations.

Administrators are also demonstrating some advanced technology skills by participating in webinars (66 percent) and professional online communities (60 percent).

As can be seen, the winds are shifting towards digital connections in education. Students, teachers and administrators are all going there, which seems to be a natural progression since the advent of the Internet. How do their statistics translate into action for education?

## Highlights

Two-thirds of teachers are taking advantage of school portals and uploading class information to keep students and parents informed about grades, homework and class activities. Teachers are also on the vanguard of social networking with regular updates to their personal profiles (45 percent); only 29 percent of administrators are part of the Facebook crowd today. *Source: http://www.tomorrow.org/ speakup/pdfs/SU10_3EofEducation_Educators.pdf*

Additionally, the use of adaptive technology shows solid promise. In August 2011, SRI International published an independent study that showed students' test scores improved by 5.5 percent a year using the adaptive math program DreamBox for 16 weeks. *Source:*

*http://www.fastcoexist.com/1678951/what-three-big-edtechinvestments-say-about-the-future-of-education*

The Facebook revolution is being applied at the academic level. Some 10 million teachers and students now have Edmodo accounts (a Facebook-like platform for students and teachers), up from 500,000 in September 2010. Students and teachers can connect from anywhere on a platform they are already familiar with. *Source: http://www.fastcoexist.com/1678951/what-three-big-edtech-investments-say-aboutthe-future-of-education*

Here's something else to think about: according to Cambridge, Mass.-based Forrester Research, 20 percent of U.S. millionaires never attended college. Further, the average net worth of billionaires who dropped out of college ($9.4 billion) is more than double that of Ph.D. billionaires ($3.2 billion). It would be irresponsible and an omission in facts to advocate that, if you want to be rich, drop out of school, or that somehow school does not matter, or that school is more of a hindrance to the genius mind than it is a help. However, the point here is, shouldn't our schools and post-secondary institutions be a safe environment for out-of-the-box thinkers, the world's greatest innovators, rebels and artists? Shouldn't they be incubators that nurture the best in us? If schools were customized, personalized and tailored to the student, then would they not always and consistently be a place for great minds to flourish and prosper toward the highest levels of success?

## NCLB vs. NCHB
Under the NCLB model, even with the best intentions, the demand that "no child be left behind" meant that slower students hinder the advancement of the entire group, seriously limiting opportunities for average and above-average students. Brushing aside the aptitude of individual learners at the expense of average, advanced and gifted students could also be felt in the standardization of academic weakness promulgated by the NCLB approach, where states began setting lower standards for testing in order to comply with the law. Lowering the bar led to delusions of academic improvements, and true academic excellence began to be lost among all the standardized testing and threats of losing funding. Further, 'top-performing' schools in states with lax standards got manic in the face of success only to crash and burn in an international arena.

Focused squarely on the individual learner, the No Child Held Back approach does not ignore student aptitude. NCHB advocates for the standardization of academic strength through personalized, customized learning made more possible through maturing educational technologies and pushes for a curriculum in which authentic learning is happening every day at the student level.

Indeed, an NCHB approach nurtures a student (as well as parents, administrators and educational leadership) out of a single-track, sorted, tiered-student mindset (think learning disabled, academically challenged lower-level learners and assorted 'flunking' students to middle-of-the-road, mediocre, making-it, 'average-to-good' or 'B' level students, to academically advanced, advanced placement, gifted students).

All of this conveyor-belt, "sort them out" school-as-a-factory mentality should have ended when the last Model-T Ford drove off the line. However, it did not. Now, it will. The old mindset, the old factory model no longer serves us. Students, parents, teachers, educational leaders and even business leaders are all screaming for a new kind of education.

To continue to push students through an antiquated system that no longer serves them and possibly never did is a grave crime that we will pay for. Billions have been spent on special education and mentally disadvantaged students, yet just a fraction has been spent on gifted and talented students. And, ironically, neither population is winning. With an NCHB approach, this spending structure begins to naturally equalize because all students will have access to exactly what they need.

A customized, individualized learning approach is made possible through matching personal technology tools that help both the learner who processes information more slowly (usually referred to as students with special needs) as well as the learners who tend to process more rapidly (usually referred to as gifted and talented learners). Keep in mind that learning is not a race. There is no time-based competition and there is no problem with having different levels of abilities in different areas accessed at different speeds. *All* students are gifted in their own right. Each and every one of us has something special to tap into; we simply need a system that will allow this! What is important is that each student be allowed to reach his or her own personal goals at his or her own pace. "Fast" and "slow" are not the main considerations. Reaching academic goals with a purpose (or purposes) should be the focus.

In fact, such labels begin to fall away as we realize it was never the student but *the system* that was at fault. Labeling the student was a disservice to the student, when the reality was that the system was not equipped to accommodate their learning style, the attention they required or the level they were at—whatever level that may have been.

Times are changing, and education is now changing, too.

One of the most important realizations those involved with schools must have is that, if old mindsets and ingrained habits die hard, then it is better to get out of the way and allow for change to happen rather than to block the inevitable changes that must occur in order for the system to morph into a new kind of system that truly serves each and every student on a personal level.

## A Few Guidelines

Allowing students to move at their own pace, catch up to their peers, and explore broader bodies of knowledge after mastering basic proficiency requirements requires easy-to-use learning tools. Teachers must be able to quickly and easily set up learning programs for either remedial instruction or enhanced exploration.

Students must have engaging digital content that gives them a sense of where they are in relation to mastery, and offers them powerful tools for learning what they have yet to learn. This puts students in the driver's seat of their own education.

Parents need access to these tools so they can guide their children and assess progress throughout the school year. Involving parents will help to motivate students to apply themselves to their studies. Methods and techniques to motivate will depend upon the age of the student and the subject.

This approach also requires built-in assessments, or tests, used to indicate where improvement is needed. Ultimately, the test should allow each student to ask and answer, *"How much of my potential have I fulfilled?"* Using these measures with potential as their focus, parents will be equipped to help their students succeed based upon the personality and capabilities of the individual.

Finally, administrators need to assess learning progress across schools and districts. As these tools continue to develop and mature, all of this is becoming increasingly possible—and increasingly widespread.

Now more than at any other point in our history, we are closer to being able to make education personalized for the student, simpler for the teacher to plan—and more effective to the benefit of the individual, as much as to society.

No Child Held Back ™

## NOTES

## Consider This

1. What does personalized digital learning mean to you?

2. In the classrooms you see, where is there evidence of personalized learning? What are some ways that these classrooms can improve?

3. How is personalized learning a part of the system in your school district? What are some ways that your district can improve?

4. In what ways could your school do more personalized learning?

5. What advice would you give others who are looking to personalize learning?

6. How is it possible to take your school from the existing mode of operation and ramp it up so that personalized learning is a key part of a transformed approach to student achievement?

No Child Held Back™

## NOTES

_____

_____

_____

_____

_____

_____

_____

_____

_____

_____

_____

_____

_____

_____

_____

_____

**For Your Exploration**

1. Observe a classroom to see where personalized learning is taking place. Take notes on what you see.

2. Ask a student how what they are learning in class relates to their interests, talents and goals.

3. Find out what technologies are accessible, possibly free, that assist with personalized learning.

No Child Held Back™

## NOTES

_____

_____

_____

_____

_____

_____

_____

_____

_____

_____

_____

_____

_____

_____

_____

_____

## Already On It

Tom Vander Ark, www.GettingSmart.com
Bob Wise, www.all4ed.org
Susan Patrick, http://www.inacol.org/
Elliot Washor, http://www.bigpicture.org/
School of One, schoolofone.org
StudyBlue, www.studyblue.com
Knewton, www.knewton.com
BrainPop, www.brainpop.com

## Recommended Reading

*Getting Smart: How Digital Learning is Changing the World.* Vander Ark, 2011.

*The Learning Edge.* Bain and Weston, 2011.

*Blogs, Wikis, Podcasts and Other Powerful Web Tools for Classrooms.* Richardson, 2010.

*Disrupting Class: How Disruptive Innovation Will Change the Way the World Learns.* Christensen, Johnson and Horn, 2008.

*Teaching with the Tools Kids Really Use: Learning With Web and Mobile Technologies.* Brooks-Young, 2010.

## Talking Points

1. In essentially every other facet of our lives, we have choice. Each human being is also built differently. Why not create a set of tools that matches our essential uniqueness in education?

When we buy a car, we look for the features that will work for our lifestyle. When we choose foods to eat, we make choices, hopefully, based on the kinds and combinations of food that will support our overall health and well-being. Our eyes are different, our fingerprints are different, we think differently, we come from different walks of life. Why, then would we submit ourselves to educational tools that treat us like we are all the same? We need to have a choice in teachers, content, paths of learning, and modes of learning. Just like in the other facets of our lives, choice here will allow us to be at our personal best.

2. Personalized learning tools shift the responsibility for learning to the student.

When students are able to self-select courses within a given framework and their own methods of learning established objectives, they are in the driver's seat of their own learning. This also allows them the ability to challenge themselves.

In addition, students live in a world where things happen "on my terms, not your terms." Burger King implores us to have our Whopper hamburgers our way. DVRs allow us to tape our favorite shows and watch them when it works for us. Facebook is set up so that we determine who we will friend and who can see what. And the list goes on.

Students living in this world may become resistant to an education system that, in their perception, says "you have no choice here." By offering them choice through personalized learning tools, they have a far greater chance of feeling empowered to engage in their own education.

No Child Held Back ™

## NOTES

_____

_____

_____

_____

_____

_____

_____

_____

_____

_____

_____

_____

_____

_____

_____

_____

YOVEL BADASH

7

# THE CONTENT MARKETPLACE

**The educational content** marketplace is wide open right now. There are so many options for moving public schools toward the NCHB model. Content aggregators are interested in partnering with leading individuals and/or companies worldwide who can offer high-quality educational content. These aggregators then redistribute it, often establishing unique meeting places (high-traffic hub sites) for content owners, students, educators and institutions.

Such aggregators look to expand the diversity of their collections, pushing the boundaries to improve quality, to increase quantity, and to ensure that the content is engaging, relevant, attractive and easily navigable. The content itself must be in a format that is online-friendly, and aligned to Common Core standards (or other local standards). The value and benefits of using a content aggregator include easier access to the general market and, of course, revenue generation from the content owner's perspective.

Stepping back a bit, content owners and content creators are challenged with how they can get *to* the market. They ask questions such as, should I sell to schools directly? What is the most effective route forward? Should I create a destination site? How do I get traffic? Who are the right partners in terms of reselling or representation? How can I think global and still be local?

The rules of the marketplace are changing, especially within just the last few years. Easy access to the target market of educators, educational institutions and directly to learners is a game with shifting rules and new opportunities. As with any business, visibility, traction and a following are key components in the content marketplace. For example, companies like Coursera offer free online university level courses and boast partnerships with thirty-three of some of the nation's most prestigious universities. Another example is EdX, a not-for-profit enterprise. Co-founded by Harvard University and the Massachusetts Institute of Technology, it features learning designed specifically for interactive study via the Web. Based on a long history of collaboration and their shared educational missions, the founding universities are creating a new online-learning experience with online courses that reflect their disciplinary breadth. Along with offering online courses, the institutions will use EdX to research how students learn and how technology can transform learning–both on-campus and worldwide.

From a content provider's perspective, a transparent marketplace reveals who gets paid and how much they get compensated. When a consumer (teacher, student, school district, etc.) licenses or purchases content, the best aggregators will automatically pay the content owner.

Aggregators deal with individuals, groups, schools, districts and even on the state level. They provide support and assist in positioning and marketing their content providers, and work to improve SEO and conversion statistics. Let's take a look at some of the specifics.

### Statistics

The content marketplace is alive and well. The Education Division of the Software and Information Industry Association (SIIA), the principal trade association for the software and digital content industries, recently released the *2010 U.S. Educational Technology Industry Market: PreK-12 Report*. First in a series of SIIA market reports, the survey values the overall market PreK-12 non-hardware educational technology at $7.5 billion —with content-related products representing 42 percent of that revenue.

To better understand the size and scope of the market, analysts used survey results and publicly available data. They divided products into four segments:
-content
-instructional support
-platforms and
-administrative tools.

A special segment included advanced placement, special education, and English language learner materials. The study did not include print, hardware or analog products—instead, it focused only on revenues for software and digital content or resources, and institutional sales—to paint a picture of the overall revenue of educational technology companies. The report presents the results of a supply-side survey of publishers, developers, and service providers and aggregates the sector's digital revenues in the pre-K-12 market.

"The inaugural report comes at a time when the national conversation around 'ed-tech' has unprecedented attention, and when our educational system is aggressively making the transition to digital," said report author John Richards, Ph.D. "Now is the time to provide industry stakeholders a focused look at this promising subsection of a sprawling and complicated market."

Ambient Insight also compiled information about mobile learning into the report *The US Market for Mobile Learning Products and Services: 2010-2015 Forecast and Analysis*. In this report, it is found that the U.S. is now the top country for buying mobile learning such as online courses and educational phone apps, followed by Japan, South Korea, Great Britain and Taiwan. It is forecasted that the U.S. will remain the top buyer for the next several years as well.

### Highlights
A lot of materials, activities, lesson plans, resources, applications and content already exist. Each classroom, school and school district needs to be able to bring these great content elements and courses to the forefront. We call it a 'marketplace' very deliberately —it *needs* to be a marketplace. Each educational organization needs to have the ability to create and use relevant content that fits *their specific situation*. For example, if in a certain area in New York, there

is an issue with math for elementary students—then they need to create a supporting marketplace that would be open to all and that focused on this area. The marketplace should be available for use by schools and parents—and it should be an active, vibrant environment that adjusts to the local realities and constraints.

There are many questions that need to be answered as this is new territory. Some wonder whether or not teachers should be able to sell their lesson plans online and—if they can—whether they should give their school district a cut. Are lesson plans copyrighted materials for the teachers who create them, or school property— even if they were teacher created? Does selling lessons online demean the value of teacher responsibilities? There are many discussions, but not many answers at this time. Although copyright issues have yet to be sorted out, why reinvent the wheel if you are able to access great lessons plans online, especially if it saves you hours each week?

## The content marketplace and NCHB

How is the content marketplace important to NCHB? Extending access to content beyond the inherently limited resources of a single class, a local school, or even a single school district opens a world of new opportunities. No single textbook company or content provider can deliver the breadth of options that an entire ecosystem of education partners can offer. NCHB framework technologies must support access to many sources of content in order for teachers and parents to select the optimal resources for each student.

**Student-centered learning.** Being able to source high quality content from sources all over the world to fit the specific needs of each school and that focus on student-centered learning is one of the best qualities of the content marketplace. No matter whether the school is already top performing and intends to remain that way or is a school with severe budget cuts, each school district should be able to find the correct content for their specific needs.

**World-class content.** Delivered electronically or in blended learning environments, world-class content is a powerful tool for normalizing instructional quality in schools with high numbers of inexperienced or under qualified teachers—particularly lower-performing inner-city schools. Content can also be rated on some aggregators by previous users, giving the upper hand to the consumer before investing in anything that may not be high enough quality.

**Common Core standards.** The educational content marketplace, when aligned with Common Core standards, is a key component to the NCHB philosophy. These standards allow for the flexibility needed to provide individual pathways for each student while defining the skills and content needed to smoothly transition into postsecondary study or the workforce. Of course, the entire idea behind the Common Core Standards is building upon knowledge step by step with full understanding—before moving onto the next concept (just like NCHB).

**Classwork and homework transformation.** By being able to choose an already high-quality, proven curriculum, teachers are able to concentrate more on the progress of each student rather than on curriculum creation and intense lesson planning. Additionally, the structure of the class changes as students study concepts at home or on their own, and are able to practice concepts during class time rather than the other way around.

By having access to quality content online, teachers are able to expand perspectives to students unlike ever before. Instead of one source for content, why not many—if they are reputable? And if you have great-quality curriculum, why not share it online and make a few extra bucks in the meantime?

Perhaps the greatest value of a content marketplace is its ability to level the playing field around the world. Whether residing in rural West Africa or Midtown Manhattan, each school and district will have access to the very best content possible at very low costs. In addition, schools can offer *any* type of course or program to address a child's particular interests and needs.

It is no longer necessary, for example, to hire a home economics teacher in order for a child to learn how to cook. A child drawn to cooking can learn the basics through a course online and practice right there in his kitchen at home. A child who is interested in studying about another country can take a class about that country online, whether or not the country is included in her core social studies and political science curriculum. Under this paradigm and with these tools in place, "career exploration" takes on a whole new meaning!

Indeed, the doors are wide open in a content marketplace. We are more equipped than ever before to provide a rich learning environment where children can explore interests to which they are uniquely drawn! Can you imagine what will be possible when, say, a young child with a love of music who happens to live in East Mississippi, one of the most impoverished areas in the world—has access to courses in jazz, classical piano, musicology, and songwriting online? Or the child who is excelling in the basics and has a love of drawing can learn art from some of the world's most renowned artists through an online course?

With rich content in place, drawn from the greatest minds and talents across the world, we will continue to grow a world full of great minds and talents. No longer will parents sit at the dinner table and hear their children complain about how bored they are in school. Quite the contrary—it will be hard for parents to get their children to stop talking!

*This* is the vision of NCHB: joyful, excited learners who are discovering what they are strong in and drawn to and pursuing that with a passion.

In this wide world of open opportunity, what do you have to contribute? What would you create if you had the tools and platform to do it? Who would you want to touch? This is ever-more in your reach. To learn more, visit www.nochildheldback.com

## Already On It

www.khanacademy.org
www.namaya.com
www.educationtogo.com
www.schooltube.com
www.youtube.com/education
www.teacherspayteachers.com
www.acquirecontent.com/e-learning
www.brainpop.com

## Recommended Reading

*Dancing with Digital Natives: Staying in Step with the Generation That's Transforming the Way Business is Done.* Manafy and Gautschi.

## A Few Guidelines

1. Who is in charge of procuring content in your organization?

2. What criteria are used in content selection? Who selects content?

3. What options do you have when it comes to access to quality educational content?

4. What are some examlples of high-quality education content and what makes them excellent?

5. Do you think the content marketplace should be local or not—and why or why not?

6. What advantages or disadvantages do you see with a content marketplace? What are the benefits that a marketplace provides?

No Child Held Back™

## NOTES

_____

_____

_____

_____

_____

_____

_____

_____

_____

_____

_____

_____

_____

_____

_____

_____

## For Your Consideration

1. Where do you currently get your content?
2. Are you happy with the quality of your content? Why or why not?
3. What are the costs involved in obtaining premium content? Are there ways to defray those costs?
4. What are the benefits and drawbacks of a self-contained content provider?
5. What other considerations do you have about obtaining high-quality content?

No Child Held Back ™

## NOTES

_____

_____

_____

_____

_____

_____

_____

_____

_____

_____

_____

_____

_____

_____

_____

_____

## For Your Exploration

Imagine what it would be like to use content found online from multiple sources but based around teaching specific topics.

Do you think it would be more diverse or limiting, than using textbooks and a few supportive materials?

How do you think students would respond to it? Would it make a teacher's life easier or harder?

How would it change your role as a student, teacher, educational administrator, community member, or business stakeholder?

No Child Held Back ™

## NOTES

_____

_____

_____

_____

_____

_____

_____

_____

_____

_____

_____

_____

_____

_____

_____

_____

## Notable

The Common Core standards differ from NCLB in that standards are not targeted at the lowest common denominator but were rather designed by some of the top minds in the country—one key component of all top-performing countries.

The overall market for pre-K-12 non-hardware educational technology is estimated at $7.5 billion—with content-related products representing 42 percent of that revenue.

The U.S. is currently the top buyer of mobile learning materials—more than Japan, South Korea and Taiwan.

## Talking Points

1. The Content Marketplace levels the playing field. When high-quality content and instructional methods are available through open source systems, every teacher and every child has access to the best available content for their current unit of study. No longer does a student in rural North Carolina, for example, have to resign themselves to the fact that they will get a lower quality education than their peers living in the highest income tax brackets in the same state.

The content marketplace opens up healthy competition, which lends itself to high-quality products—and ingenuity.

2. People want to have their personally-designed content selected for use. Because there is so much available in the marketplace, content providers take care to research their work and provide the best available. This system of healthy competition leads to ingenuity and innovation, leaving educational consumers with a wide array of high-quality material from which to choose.

No Child Held Back™

## NOTES

_____

_____

_____

_____

_____

_____

_____

_____

_____

_____

_____

_____

_____

_____

_____

_____

_____

YOVEL BADASH

# 8
# CONTENT CREATION TOOLS

**It used to** be the case that publishing was squarely in the realm of the elite. Increasingly, we live in an always-on world where everyone is capable of creating content and sharing it. Content creation tools and resources are now available for free or near-free to anyone who looks. With computer or mobile access, such tools are democratizing the content business, and they are empowering students and teachers to become content creators and publishers.

Days of mass consumers and elite publishers as the only providers are numbered. Sure, there's a spectrum ranging from amateur to professional, where quality of content improves on a gradient. But the contrast is no longer a sharp divide, and it is wide open for the making, if you choose to create it. Quality will always sort itself out along the way, and the Internet 'crowds' often have a way of seeing real value.

As for education in particular, when a teacher creates a new course, worksheet, activity, problem set or other teaching resource, preserving those efforts within a digital delivery system can multiply the value of that teacher's hard work across many students and classes. Leveraging the value of each teacher's time and expertise is crucial to the success of No Child Held Back. *Value multipliers*, such as the ability to easily find, create, share, and reuse content—are a key technology requirement.

Content creation is a rather large category, but there are many ways to approach the area. Here are a few different systems that assist in providing a platform for content creation:

-Virtual learning environments,
-Content management systems, and
-Learning management systems.

There are literally hundreds of content creation tools. They fall into some familiar categories, depending on the media and/or purpose of your activities. Some of the more common ones include:
Aggregators
Collaboration tools
Online applications
Photo sharing
Podcasting
Presentation tools
Social networking
Utilities
Video sharing
Research tools
Slideshow tools
Audio tools
Image tools
Drawing tools
Writing tools
Music tools
Organizing tools
Converting tools
Mapping tools
Quiz tools
Poll tools
Graphing tools
Creativity tools
Widgets
File storage and
Web tools.

There are broader tools available in the content creation sphere, including learning management systems (LMS). LMS has a variety of definitions, but a simple way of looking at it is as *a software application that administers, documents, tracks and reports all classroom and online learning programs and content.* An LMS usually has a number of benefits, including enabling centralization and automation of administration; helping to assemble and deliver learning content rapidly; consolidating academic programs on a scalable web platform; it supports portability and standards; personalizing content and enables knowledge to be re-used.

Although there are many more, a few content creation and management tools we wanted to mention are:

Moodle.org
NaMaYa.com
Equella.com
Microsoft Sharepoint
Blackboard/WebCT
Sakai (sakaiproject.org)
LAMS Foundation (lamsfoundation.org)
eCampus.com
Pearson Learning Solutions (pearsonlearningsolutions.com)

All of these tools literally have the ability to streamline the content creation process so that the focus can be on quality. Something that used to take teachers hours to prepare can now take much less time —and can be shared.

YouTube for Schools is a setting where teachers and administrators can gain access to hundreds of thousands of educational-only videos about topics in many subjects. Partners include: Smithsonian, TED, Steve Spangler Science and Numberphile, among roughly *600 other* content providers. Google is also working with teachers to create more than 300 'playlists' of helpful videos sorted by subject and grade level. This should help in the fight against Annoying Orange, cute kittens, funny babies, Justin Bieber and other massively popular distractions—to keep students focused on the task at hand.

Whether you have all of the content creation tools you need or not, there are also plenty of companies that supply enough content to help you make your way forward.

There are many content suppliers online, but here are a few highlights in no particular order:

*PBS Teachers* is PBS' national web destination for quality pre-K-12 resources where you can find classroom materials for various subjects and grade levels. Thousands of lesson plans, teaching activities, on-demand video assets, and interactive games and simulations are correlated to state and national standards. They're often associated with NOVA, Nature, Cyberchase, Between the Lions and other PBS shows. www.pbs.org/teachers

*TeachersPayTeachers* is an online marketplace where teachers buy and sell original educational materials, goods and/or used educational resources. It's a place where teachers who are content creators have in some cases made well over $100,000. Those are extreme cases, but it goes to show how quality content creation, distribution, and current Internet technology can go a long way toward meeting a demand. www.teacherspayteachers.com

*Adobe* is a key company in the area of content creation tools. It helps educators prepare their students by providing tools for the development of digital communication and creativity skills needed in today's job force. They offer standards-aligned curricula, certification, professional development and flexible purchasing programs. No matter the size of the school, it is ensured that students are set up for success. In K-12, Adobe promotes literacy, teaches essential career skills, facilitates online learning and helps to streamline administrative processes. www.adobe.com/education.html

With content creation and management tools, educators can deliver rich online training content for staff development with built-in tracking and assessment; content can go paperless with digital forms including report cards, parent bulletins, records and academic resources; and archiving is made easier as well. Robust content management and digital analytic tools assist with knowledge management, Web experience management and general collaboration and productivity in both K-12 and higher education settings.

From podcasts and screencasts, to suites of content creation products, Google Docs, YouTube, SchoolTube and many other approaches will help move you forward in creating and sharing content, empowering you to reach out beyond your classroom, your school and your city to assist others on an unlimited, global level.

## Stats

"Content is king" has usually meant that if you expect to be successful in any venture, then the quality of your content must be a top priority. Education is awash in content, but is it our top priority? And is it of the highest quality available anywhere? It should be. However, it usually isn't and that is often a top complaint among educators, students, parents and anyone in and around education. Nonetheless, that doesn't mean that professional content providers all the way down to user-generated "content providers" haven't tried to make it better, either with money or sheer social media enthusiasm.

The Education Division of the Software and Information Industry Association (SIIA), the principle trade association for the software and digital content industries, recently released the *2010 U.S. Educational Technology Industry Market: PreK-12 Report*. First in a series of SIIA market reports, the survey values the overall market PreK-12 non-hardware educational technology at $7.5 billion—with *content*-related products representing 42 percent of that revenue.

According to Pew Internet and American Life Project data looking at "networked creators" among Internet users, 65 percent are social networking users. What are they doing? Fifty-five percent are sharing photos, 30 percent are sharing personal creations, 26 percent are posting comments on sites and blogs, 15 percent have their own personal website, 15 percent are "content remixers," 14 percent are bloggers, and 13 percent use Twitter.

Overall, *user-generated* content is on the rise. Below is a list of year-to-year projections going back to 2008 of the percent of U.S. Internet users who have contributed content online and what researchers anticipate Web users will contribute in the future:

2008: 42.8 %
2009: 44.6 %

2010: 46.6 %
2011: 48.2 %
2012: 50.0 %
2013: 51.8 %

*Source: Tech Crunchies – Internet Statistics and Numbers*

As for digital content in the classroom, what are teachers using and librarians recommending? Librarians most highly recommend real-time data (40 percent); followed by skill development software (39 percent); podcasts and videos (38 percent); virtual field trips (31 percent); online textbooks (19 percent); animations, simulations and games (16 percent) and virtual labs (11 percent). *Source: Project Tomorrow*

## Highlights
One important aspect to address before moving on is that content, whether you make it yourself or find it elsewhere, should follow the Common Core learning standards. To date, 44 states already have adopted these standards, which were created as a way to clearly define what it is that our students need to know in order to succeed in college and the workplace, both locally and on a global scale.

The design of the standards is like that of a spiral staircase, going up and up, building upon step after step and returning to the same subject only one level up each year. These standards were informed by top-performing countries and determined among a collaboration of the National Governors Association Center for Best Practices, the Council of Chief State School Officers, teachers, school administrators, and other experts.

With these standards in place, all students will have had access to the same topics no matter where they live. Common Core standards build upon certain steps that should be taken starting in kindergarten that ultimately lead to certain outcomes by the end of high school in order to prepare students for vocational school, college or career. How are these different than other standards? They help serve as *guidelines*—rather than restrictive requirements—and are easily modified to fit the needs of individual students.

Common Core learning standards are provided for each year and each subject for pre-Kindergarten through 12, making them a valuable tool to have at hand when creating your own content or finding already existing content.

## NCLB vs. NCHB

In the old school model encouraged under NCLB, teachers must keep up with learning objectives as they might be found on tests. Adequate Yearly Progress (AYP) meant glossing over loads of information, and mile-wide, inch-deep learning seemed to be the only way to realistically keep up; although in practice, it turned out not to be so realistic at all.

NCHB, on the other hand, advocates for flipping that model through transformative technologies that free up students and teachers to engage in authentic, often constructivist based learning activities and projects that feed into a portfolio of accumulating evidence tying directly to the interests, talents and goals of the individual learner. While these may be *aligned* to Common Core learning standards, they are not *dictated* by them. With NCHB, a teacher's time is valued, as is their expertise. Both of these can be helped by leveraging the value of technological tools to address content creation, sharing and re-using for the direct benefit of the individual learner in a student-centric learning environment.

## A Few Guidelines

Content creation tools should be intuitive and easy to use in addition to providing for the needs of teachers and administrators. Those listed in this chapter fit this description, but keep this in mind if you find another tool.

When finding quality supplied content, read reviews from others before purchasing.

Also ask the opinions of the people who will actually be using the tools.

And lastly – don't be afraid to experiment. If you don't try you will never know what is possible.

No Child Held Back ™

## NOTES

## For Your Consideration

1. What percentage of your classroom content is original content? Where is the majority of your classroom content coming from?

2. When is the last time you surveyed your class/child regarding interests, talents and goals? Take some time to do that in the near future.

3. What projects might you take on, that feed into the interests, talents and goals of your students?

4. What free content creation tools exist to improve student learning? How often do you use them?

5. Have your students generate a list of content providers and sources. Which ones surprise you?

6. What does your school year look like in terms of digital and other content?

7. What would the ideal content creation tool do for your classroom?

8. What part does content creation play in a school district?

No Child Held Back™

## NOTES

**For Your Exploration**

Research:

What are the best content creation tools out there?

How do they meet the needs of your students?

How do these tools meet administrative, tracking, assessment, and reporting needs?

No Child Held Back™

## NOTES

_____

_____

_____

_____

_____

_____

_____

_____

_____

_____

_____

_____

_____

_____

_____

_____

## Already On It

SIIA
Big Ideas Learning
Carnegie Learning
NaMaYa
CourseSites from Blackboard
Six Red Marbles
Edison Learning
Curriculum Associates
Key Curriculum Press
Evan-Moor Educational Publishers
Pearson
Saxon from Houghton Mifflin Harcourt
Teacher Created Materials
Scholastic
Teacher Created Resources
McGraw-Hill Companies
Khan Academy
Study Island
Discovery Education
AdaptEDMind
Adaptive Curriculum
Destination Math
Virtual Nerd

## Recommended Reading

*Dancing with Digital Natives: Staying in Step with the Generation That's Transforming the Way Business is Done.* Manafy and Gautschi.

*Disrupting Class: How Disruptive Innovation Will Change the Way the World Learns.* Clayton M. Christensen.

## Talking Points

1. Content creation tools allow teachers the freedom to customize.

Teachers know what their students need. Through user-friendly tools, teachers can refine and tweak available content, or develop brand new content that meets specific learning goals and specific learning styles of the students they are serving.

2. Content creation tools allow teachers the freedom to share, thus saving time and energy.

Many states are now adopting a "common core" of state-wide standards. Teachers are developing lessons and units based on these standards.

Content creation tools, within an open source framework, would allow a North Carolina English Language Arts teacher seeking the best methods for teaching "Standard One" access to all the materials developed by teachers across the state, or even across the country.

This keeps the teacher from having to think through the best approaches alone. It also keeps her from taking time to reinvent the wheel. Time can now be spent on facilitating the learning process for every child.

No Child Held Back™

## NOTES

_____

_____

_____

_____

_____

_____

_____

_____

_____

_____

_____

_____

_____

_____

_____

_____

_____

_____

YOVEL BADASH

# 9

# ROBUST PROFESSIONAL DEVELOPMENT

**Teachers are the** key to any educational reform. They are a huge power and represent a high percentage of the workforce. But the reality is that, other than getting their education degrees (B.A. or M.A.), ongoing professional development for teachers could be far better. The same NCHB logic we apply to students should be applied to teachers.

If one teacher has great skills in one area, but is challenged in another, then he or she must be able to develop and learn the missing areas. In regards to professional development of a teacher, we must change the way teachers think, the way they are evaluated and the way they are managed. We must allow them to focus on teaching and inspiring kids.

Meanwhile, each school or school district needs to have its own customized professional development solution—its own "teacher effectiveness" platform. If helping teachers excel is fundamental to improving students' immediate and long-term learning outcomes, it is crucial for schools and districts to provide a strong set of convenient, cost-effective professional development resources for teachers and administrators. A recent McKinsey study of school systems that have achieved sustained improvement over time explains that school systems have different intervention requirements for success depending on their starting point. Professional development at each transition point is an integral part of the transformation management that is needed to make lasting improvements in our schools.

Educators looking for professional development resources on the Web have it much different than they did a decade ago. In 2000, resources such as the how-to, video-rich Atomic Learning were just beginning. It was started by a couple of guys editing helpful content out of a garage in Wisconsin who were forced to provide short snippets to combat universally low-bandwidth situations. Facebook wouldn't even come online for another four years, and the majority of the resources listed on the next few pages just didn't exist.

Now in 2012, the professional development scene for teachers has advanced quite a bit, though we can't really call it mature just yet. Consider it (somewhat arbitrarily) as you might a 10-year-old: sure signs of precociousness, lots of potential—but still not fully grown up.

Nonetheless, there are enough great resources out there to make the web a true gift to educators looking for help. There are plenty of excellent online professional development resources to help move you toward a true 21$^{st}$ century classroom.

**Statistics**

How is technology being used by teachers both in the classroom and elsewhere? It is actually already quite prevalent in many schools with the exception of those that are low income. Consider these key findings on teachers' use of educational technology in public schools during the winter and spring of 2009 (Source: *Teachers' Use of Educational Technology in U.S. Public Schools: 2009 Selected Findings* from the National Center for Education Statistics).

Ninety-seven percent of teachers had one or more computers located in the classroom every day, while 54 percent could bring computers into the classroom. Internet access was available for 93 percent of the computers located in the classroom every day and for 96 percent of the computers that could be brought into the classroom. Teachers reported that they or their students used computers in the classroom during instructional time often (40 percent) or sometimes (29 percent). Teachers also reported that they or their students used computers in other locations in the school during instructional time often (29 percent) or sometimes (43 percent).

What *kinds* of technology are available and in use? Teachers reported having the following technology devices either available as needed or in the classroom every day: LCD (liquid crystal display) or DLP (digital light processing) projectors (36 and 48 percent, respectively), interactive whiteboards (28 and 23 percent), and digital cameras (64 and 14 percent).

Of the teachers with the device available, the percentage that used it sometimes or often for instruction was 72 percent for LCD or DLP projectors, 57 percent for interactive whiteboards, and 49 percent for digital cameras.

Teachers indicated that a system on their school or district network was available for entering or viewing the following: grades (94 percent), attendance records (93 percent), and results of student assessments (90 percent).

Of the teachers with one of these systems available, the percentage using it sometimes or often was 92 percent (grades), 90 percent (attendance records), and 75 percent (student assessments).

Of the teachers who participated in technology-related professional development during the 12 months prior to completing the survey, 81 percent agreed that it met their goals and needs; 88 percent agreed that it supported the goals and standards of their state, district, and school; 87 percent agreed that it applied to technology available in their school; and 83 percent agreed that it was available at convenient times and places.

Upon closer scrutiny of the Department of Education report, the findings are actually much more complex. They reveal some very interesting disparities in technological access between affluent and low-income schools.

Differences were found for the percentage of teachers who sometimes or often did the following: used email or list-serve to send out group updates or information to parents (69 percent compared to 39 percent) or to students (30 percent compared to 17 percent), used email to address individual concerns with parents (92 percent compared to 48 percent) or with students (38 percent compared to 19 percent), used a course or teacher web page to communicate with parents (47 percent compared to 30 percent) or with students (36 percent compared to 18 percent).

Results also differed between high and low income schools for the percentage of teachers that reported that their students used educational technology sometimes or often during classes to prepare written text (66 and 56 percent, respectively), learn or practice basic skills (61 and 83 percent), and develop and present multimedia presentations (47 and 36 percent).

Poverty concentration is based on the percent of students eligible for free or reduced-price lunch (less than 35 percent and 75 percent or more—referred to as low and high poverty, respectively). *Source: National Center for Education Statistics*

What can we extrapolate from all of this information? That while technology is already in use in many schools, it is not being fully *utilized* in schools, whether high or low income. There is much more that can be accomplished and better ways of using what's already available. Professional development can enhance the use of these technological tools both to the benefit of teachers and students.

## Highlights

In March 2011, ASCD was awarded a $3 million grant by the Bill & Melinda Gates Foundation to support implementation of Common Core learning standards over a three-year period. ASCD's efforts include a series of meetings supporting the transition to the new Common Core standards in selected states. These meetings will disseminate information about the new standards, as well as gather feedback from educators about what they need to help bring the standards to life through effective classroom instruction.

Some districts such as Mt. Airy City Schools in North Carolina, plan on providing all of their teachers with laptops. Such a move is intended to streamline how efficiently teachers perform their daily tasks and to help provide opportunities for professional development while implementing Common Core standards.

Another way some schools are providing professional development is through *professional learning teams,* onsite committees of teachers who meet and help each other to work collaboratively towards providing better educational opportunities for their students.

Other schools are connecting professional development programs with after-school programs such as the *EdTech Link* program through the Digital Harbor Foundation in Maryland. Benefits are two-fold: teachers first learn about new technology and then must apply it by teaching students about it.

*School Improvement Network (SINET)* is a major leader in professional development for teachers. The company offers professional development for teachers online through several outlets: their NOW In-Class Cameras, PD360, Observation 360, LiveBook 360, the Learning 360 Framework, Equity 360, and Common Core 360. PD360, for example, offers more than 1,800 high quality videos online from 120 experts. The videos feature classroom examples and are short in length, making them perfect for a quick grasp of a specific topic.

*LiveBook* is a new type of online professional development tool. Rather than one finished e-book online, authors can revise existing books so that content will remain up-to-date and can be influenced positively by input from other professionals in the field.

*NaMaYa PD* is another interesting provider, offering over 50 high quality PD courses that can be administrated by the individual district. PD leaders in these districts can then create their own PD course or edit the readymade ones to fit the specific needs of any teacher.

## NCLB vs. NCHB
Historically, administrators have favored the workshop approach where a district or school brings in an outside consultant or curriculum expert on a staff-development day to give teachers a one-time training seminar on a garden-variety pedagogic or subject-area topic. Criticized for their lack of continuity and coherence, workshops have at least in theory fallen out of favor. NCLB, for instance, defines all professional development funded through the law to include activities that "are not one-day or short-term

workshops or conferences." There is little evidence to suggest that states and districts adhere to this directive.

Even so, many teachers still appear to receive much of their professional development through some form of the one-shot workshop. Survey data from the National Center for Education Statistics, the most recent publicly available, show that in the 1999-2000 school year, 95 percent of teachers took part in workshops or training in the previous 12 months, compared with 74 percent who reported working in an instructional group and 42 percent who participated in peer observation.

A major three-part study by the Stanford Center for Opportunity Policy in Education, in partnership with the National Staff Development Council (now Learning Forward), provides some of the most up-to-date descriptive information on professional development trends in the U.S..

Released in three phases in 2009 and 2010, the study drew on a variety of sources, including reviews of mainly qualitative literature, research on teacher learning in developed countries, surveys of teachers conducted by the Learning Forward group, survey data from the annual MetLife Survey of the American Teacher, and data from three administrations of the federal Schools and Staffing Survey.

Among other findings, the reports stated that:
- Many teachers still appear to receive much of their professional development through some form of one-shot workshop.
- U.S. teachers generally spent more time instructing students and less time in professional learning opportunities with their peers than those in top-performing countries.

**Professional development.** There are many options for professional development both onsite and online. Take a moment to read about a few below and then do a little research of your own and follow "A Few Guidelines" to find the right fit for you and your school.

*PBS TeacherLine* provides professional development for educators. As a premier provider of high-quality online professional development, PBS TeacherLine has been recognized for excellence by organizations such as the U.S. Distance Learning Association, the National Educational Association, and the Software and Information Industry Association. Their collection of more than 130 top quality, graduate level courses for educators spans the entire curriculum:

Reading/Language Arts
Mathematics,
Instructional Technology,
Instructional Strategies and
Science.

Their newest offering, *PBS TeacherLine Peer Connection*, taps the power of online communication, collaboration, and content to provide a rich, flexible set of tools to help instructional coaches open and maintain productive communications and collaboration with the teachers they support.

*Intel* offers free professional development for teachers to incorporate technology into their daily lessons. This not only means how to operate technology but to also utilize it fully in order to use it for critical thinking and data analysis. The program also offers the ability for teachers to share their experiences with each other. This program has already trained more than 10 million teachers in 70 countries.

*Annenberg Learner*, a part of The Annenberg Foundation, offers free, high quality web-based video programs to promote excellent education in the US for all. These resources help teachers to become experts in their field by improving and refining their teaching methods. Annenberg Learner offers videos about specific topics for different subjects and online workshops and courses.

*ASCD* offers a slew of high quality, diverse online programs and conferences for professional development. They currently have more than 150,000 members from all levels of the educational spectrum.

There is no doubt that one of the most cost effective ways for us to improve our education system is by having better teachers. The best way to do that is investing in a teacher's PD. Once we have more highly effective teachers – we will improve education.

As stated before, a good teacher teaches three times more material than a poor performing teacher. Imagine our education system full of highly effective teachers. Some teachers would actually teach 16 or even 24 years of content within a 12-year period. Couple this approach with the other elements of the NCHB framework—and the potential for growth becomes limitless.

Districts need to evolve and provide customized personalized PD for their teachers in a way that doesn't threaten—but *empowers* teachers. The best districts would develop a self-sustained PD infrastructure that evolves to meet current and future challenges. The technology, content and best practices are already available—all we need now is to put it all together in a way that districts and teachers can benefit from—without further overwhelming them.

No matter how it is done, professional development is key to NCHB—and key to helping teachers reach their full potential.

## A Few Guidelines

1. Ensure professional development objectives are clearly stated.

2. Examine the teacher reviews of successful professional development sessions.

3. Before choosing a provider, make a list of expectations.

4. Review your successes and any need of improvement for the provider you have chosen. Share this information with them for an improved experience for all.

No Child Held Back™

## NOTES

## For Your Exploration

1. What was your best-ever experience with professional development? Why? What was your worst-ever experience? Why?

2. What is the key to quality professional development?

3. What key takeaways does all high-quality professional development require?

No Child Held Back™

## NOTES

_____

_____

_____

_____

_____

_____

_____

_____

_____

_____

_____

_____

_____

_____

_____

_____

_____

## Already On It

NaMaYa PD (namayapd.com)
Academic Merit (academicmerit.com)
LearningFront (learningfront.com)
Scholastic U (teacher.scholastic.com/products/ScholasticU)
Technology Integration in Education (TIE) (www.technologyintegrationineducation.com)
eBistro (ebistro.org/welcome/index.php)
SimpleK12 (simplek12.com and blog.simplek12.com)
Dynamite Learning (dynamitelearning.com)
LearnItIn5 (learnitin5.com)
PBSTeacherLine (www.pbs.org/teacherline)
Annenberg Learner (learner.org)
PD 360 (www.pd360.com)
Professional Learning Practice (PLP)
ASCD's PD in Focus (www.ascd.org/professional-development/pd-in-focus.aspx)
Sublime Learning (sublimelearning.com)
NCTM's PD pages (nctm.org/profdev)
NCTE (www.ncte.org)
MyLearningPlan (www.mylearningplan.com)
ETS Keeping Learning on Track (www.ets.org)
MathSolutions (mathsolutions.com)
NEA web learning (www.nea.org)
Edvantia (edvantia.org)
Atomic Learning (www.atomiclearning.com)
Adobe (www.adobe.com/education/resources/training)
Elluminate and Wimba (www.elluminate.com)
TANDBERG (www.tandberg.com)
Discovery Education (www.discoveryeducation.com/professional-development)
TeachHub (www.teachhub.com)
KnackforTeachers (knackforteachers.com)
Teachscape www.teachscape.com
Knowledge Delivery Systems www.kdsi.org

## Recommended Reading

*The Excellent Online Instructor: Strategies for Professional Development.* Palloff, Rena M.

*Transforming Professional Development into Student Results.* Reeves, Douglas B.

## Talking Points

1. Teachers want to excel; they just need to be given the means to do so.

Most teachers do not enter the profession for the money. Most teachers enter the profession because they want to have a marked impact in the quality of life of their students. Robust professional development, customized to meet each teacher's needs must be easily available to teachers to give them the tools they need to do well for their students.

2. A PD system based on technology is a cost-effective way to give teachers the best experiences available.

When budget cuts are made, often and sadly professional development is the first line item to go. Technology makes it possible to provide teachers with uncompromised high-quality experiences enabling them to acquire new ways of thinking and new skill sets, leading ultimately to student achievement.

3. Adults have different learning styles and needs, just as students do.

Under older frameworks, professional development in the U.S. has groups of teachers sit through half-day to week-long sessions where the same material is presented in the same way to everybody, but a master teacher has different needs than a first-year teacher. Also, some adults learn best visually, some kinesthetically, some auditorily, some by reading and writing. To have a real impact, our PD systems need to accommodate the varying needs of teachers with different levels of experience and different ways of internalizing and using information.

No Child Held Back ™

## NOTES

_____

_____

_____

_____

_____

_____

_____

_____

_____

_____

_____

_____

_____

_____

# YOVEL BADASH

# 10
# BROAD TECHNOLOGY ARCHITECTURE STRATEGY

**In the No** Child Held Back paradigm, learning moves beyond the boundaries of the classroom and involves numerous stakeholders in the process: students, teachers, and administrators as well as parents and the community at large. Schools and districts will need applications specifically adapted to the needs of education to support their expanded functions and interactions. Digital content management, teaching and assessment tools, email, text messaging, communication applications, volunteer and social community management tools, e-commerce systems—and other appropriate software tools must be available to support such ambitious education goals.

Any average school or school district needs an extensive network of simple, helpful supporting applications for its ongoing work. There will be a growing need for additional applications to support the NCHB framework's successful implementation. Here are some real-world examples about surveys, fundraising, communications, e-commerce and other supporting applications.

*Google Apps* (http://www.google.com/apps/intl/en/edu/) offers free email and collaboration tools for schools and the ability to extend Google Apps to meet your school's needs. The Google Apps Marketplace offers web-based applications that work seamlessly with Google Apps to enhance classroom learning, or that allows teachers to determine students' needs and select appropriate student tools, teaching aids, or administrator utilities. The Apps Marketplace helps you discover, purchase and deploy web apps that integrate with Google Apps for Education and easily integrates with other EDU platforms.

*Overview.* The Google Apps Marketplace makes it easy to extend Google Apps to meet more of your school's needs. With just a few clicks, you can discover, purchase and deploy web applications from numerous vendors that integrate with Google Apps. The Google Apps Marketplace is available for Premier, Standard, and Education editions of Google Apps.

*What are integrated apps?* Integrated apps, available in the Google Apps Marketplace, are web-based applications built by Independent Software Developers (ISVs) that connect with apps. Administrators can install integrated apps on their domains and manage them from a control panel. Once installed, integrated apps are accessible to users from Google's universal navigation bar—the links that a user sees at the top of any page—and they don't require additional logins. Upon administrator approval, some integrated apps may also read and write data to Gmail, Calendar, Docs and other Google Apps products via Google Data APIs.

*Benefits for end users.* Single sign-on. Integrated apps allow users to sign into Google Apps and securely access all available integrated apps, without additional logins or multiple passwords.

*Universal navigation.* Users can access integrated apps from the same navigation bar they use to navigate Google Apps. Users simply click the "More" drop-down located in the upper left corner of Google Apps windows.

*Data integration.* With administrator approval, integrated apps can securely access Google Apps data, eliminating information silos and redundant data and helping users work more efficiently.

*Benefits for domain administrators:*
Easy deployment; administrators can add integrated apps to their domains and enable them for users with just a few clicks without

additional licensing or the need to add on-premise hardware or software.

For those who are not familiar or comfortable with Google Apps or for those who want to expand their knowledge, there is a host of webinars available for IT and school staff.

Below are a few additional types of applications that are helpful for teachers and administrators.

**Digital content management.** This type of application helps users to manage tasks and content through storage and cataloguing and the retrieval and distribution of that digital content. Consider it an organized assistant that can work 24/7. Examples include Razuna, ResourceSpace, Evernote, and Dropbox. iCloud for Apple products is also another current example.

**Teaching and assessment tools.** There are literally hundreds of apps for phones and iPads that can assist teachers in daily tasks from taking attendance, logging grades, and creating presentations and lessons. Examples include Attendance, Flipboard, Blackboard Mobile, and PowerPresenter. As with all apps, some are free, others require a fee, but most are rated by other users and/or offer free trials.

**Email, text messaging, and other communication applications.** Communicating with students, parents and peers can be made easier through communication apps that allow for one place where multiple accounts can be read and answered. Integrating graphics and photos is also much easier than in the past. Also included is instant messaging and video chatting, both of which can allow teachers to answer students' questions during certain hours. Some are specific for Windows, others for Mac. Some also assist special education teachers in communicating better with their students. Examples include Thunderbird, PostBox 2.0, NaMaYa's EduCommunicator™, and iInteract.

**Social and community management tools.** Manage all of your social media outlets including blogs through one application. No need to log into all accounts when it all can be there in one. There are many out there, but examples include HootSuite and TweetDeck.

Schools are really a combination of different groups and communities. Students, teachers, parents and businesses around a school are just some examples of the communities that exist around any school. How can schools manage these communities? Clearly, there are many community and social management requirements schools need to deal with. Schools need to be prepared to address these needs in a flexible and scalable way.

**Other learning apps.** Students can use apps to learn just about anything or as reference sources. Some apps include dicitionary.com, Motion Math, World Wiki, and byki.

Schools, teachers, and administrators can use apps to access high-quality professional development at low cost, engage parents and the community, and connect with other like-minded professionals from around the world. At NaMaYa.com, you can find a cloud-based platform that provides content, professional development, fundraising help, parent engagement tools, and websites customized to meet your school's or district's unique needs. The platform gives your school the tools it needs to bring the focus of education back to the students.

Even with all of the great advancements in technology over the past 10 years, there may still be a few hurdles to overcome.

In 2011, McRel used the observation tool Power Walkthrough in more than 60,000 classrooms across 34 states. All demographics were covered in relation to income, race, and location. These walkthroughs were unscheduled and during different times of day.

From these walkthroughs, it was found that in 63 percent of all observations teachers were using *no technology of any kind, no matter whether the school was highly equipped with the latest technology or not.* Observations of students were equally low: 73 percent of students during Power Walkthroughs were not using any technology of any kind.

Why the discrepancy between technology availability and usage?

The majority of teachers surveyed believe that technology is not being fully utilized because of the lack of professional development and the lack of time for teachers to learn new technology tools. Source: *So Many Devices, So Little Use*, T.H.E. Journal, 6/7/2011

## Statistics

Some schools do lack the resources needed to provide adequate and up-to-date technology to their students. Low-income schools are much more likely to have resources too outdated to meet the needs of students. Thirty-four percent of public school teachers found the technology to be out of date. In low-income schools, 43 percent considered versus 30 percent in suburban areas and 33 percent in rural areas.

In schools with decreased budgets and layoffs, 39 percent of teachers reported out-of-date materials while only 22 percent said the same in schools with stable budgets.

Teachers in schools with more outdated material also reported less job satisfaction, and both teachers and parents reported feeling pessimistic about any improvements in student outcomes within the next five years (43 percent and 39 percent, respectively).

Interestingly, more parents are getting involved in their children's education with 46 percent of parents making at least one visit to their children's schools each month (compared with 16 percent in 1988). More students are also talking with their parents about school, 64 percent as compared with 40 percent in 1988. Source: *The MetLife Survey of the American Teacher: Teachers, Parents and the Economy*, 2012.

## Highlights

Despite some of the dim statistics, there are schools trying to take advantage of the latest technology in an easy-to-grasp way. For example, schools are moving towards the use of iPads or tablets in place of textbooks in all classrooms. Apple actually just recently announced the iBook 2, a digital textbook service partnership with several K-12 publishing giants. These electronic books would be offered to schools at $14.99 for each student. Sounds good, but the investment is still too steep for many schools to handle with iPads coming in at $475 apiece. Other concerns include how to control students from cruising Facebook and the Internet for non-class-related purposes.

Other school districts are opting in for free open-source textbooks, particularly attractive for school districts with tight budgets. California, for example, currently spends about $100 for each math and science textbook for its two million high school students. With open-source textbooks such as the California Open Source Textbook Project, many school districts already use laptops and tablets in place of the traditional hardbound books.

## NCLB vs. NCHB

For NCHB to be successful, teachers must have full understanding and application of online tools and apps in order to connect with students and parents in the most collaborative way possible. NCLB focused on class time—whereas the NCHB priority is getting students engaged in a way that excites them enough to want to know more. Technology is at a point where it can accomplish this. Many students already feel comfortable with an tablet, so why not incorporate it into the classroom as a centralized digital tool for study. Students can explore concepts like never before with technology. Now we need to just tie it all together with the professional development teachers need and the technological tools required.

### Long-term technology architecture strategy

Based on the broad technology and application needs listed above, it is critical schools adopt a broad and long-term technology strategy. Without taking into account the variety of technology tools and apps, schools can very quickly find themselves in front of a technology implementation, adoption and maintenance nightmare.

Technology is not the solution on its own, but a means to building the right solution. Without a long-term view and broad technology architecture strategy, the total cost of ownership of such systems would grow dramatically, while the efficacy of the technology would come into question.

Education and technology leaders need to plan for the future and design systems that are flexible and integrated so they can respond well to the changes the future will bring.

**A Few Guidelines**

1. Examine the budget at your school and what technological tools are already available.

2. Determine what advancements can be made without major monetary investments and areas where your school will have to invest.

3. Research other schools similar to yours and examine what technological improvements have been made. Then see how you can implement something similar at your school.

4. Make a list of supporting applications you would like to offer in your area. Find one provider that can address more than one item on that list.

5. Investigate opportunities for your school to receive technology grants.

No Child Held Back™

## NOTES

_____

_____

_____

_____

_____

_____

_____

_____

_____

_____

_____

_____

_____

_____

_____

_____

_____

_____

## For Your Consideration

1. How is technology, especially applications, being utilized in your classroom and at your school?

2. How do your students interact with this technology? Ask them what kind of technology they would like to begin using.

3. Of the applications you use, what are the benefits and where could they work better?

4. If technology (such as applications) is not being fully used at your school—then *why* do you think that is?

5. What would be some ways to improve the use of technology at your school?

No Child Held Back™

## NOTES

**For Your Exploration**

Determine what educational goal in your school, or your community's school, could best be supported by applications.

Research Google Apps or another supporting application (or app category) mentioned in this chapter.

How could you use the information you found to move your school or your school's community, forward in achieving its goal?

No Child Held Back ™

## NOTES

_____

_____

_____

_____

_____

_____

_____

_____

_____

_____

_____

_____

_____

_____

_____

## Already On It

There are *thousands* of providers—so many so that, to reduce them to a list here would limit your possibilities. I recommend that you do a Web search to find the best providers out there based on your needs. The best approach is to search categorically, looking for education applications in a specific target area. Here are some example target areas:

Surveys
Texting applications (to send messages to parents and community members)
Blog set up systems
Learning management systems
Website development
Marketing management
Social media management
E-commerce
Fundraising
Volunteer management and
Community management.

## Recommended Reading

*Feedback: The Hinge That Joins Teaching and Learning*, Pollock, Jane E., 2011

*Retool Your School: The Educator's Essential Guide to Google's Free Power Apps*, Lerman, James, & Hicks, Ronique, 2010

*Web 2.0: How-To for Educators*, Solomon, Gwen, & Schrum, Lynne, 2010

## Talking Points

1. To meet the needs of all its stakeholders, a school and/or school district needs to have automatic systems in place to run efficiently

A school or district can be likened to a private company. It has hundreds, thousands, or tens of thousands of customers: students, parents, community and business stakeholders. With no application strategy or technology architecture to support clear communication and engagement, schools and districts will spend far more than they need to for overhead. Also, there will be constant chaos—mixed messages, incompatible systems, and differing policies from school to school.

2. To achieve the greatest impact, schools and districts need to focus on their technology platform and overall architecture strategy.

Schools and districts often concern themselves with devices and content. Devices upgrade and content is ever-evolving. Putting emphasis on these two entities will lead to wasted energy and money. A school or district would be far better served to think about their future. What do they have now? And what do they need to move their system to be congruent with 21st-century learning and the NCHB approach? From here, schools can put together a system of technology that will be consistent and congruent.

Our investment in technology needs to be guided by a long term strategy.

We can't just think about what we need today—but what we will need in five years. Schools and districts often focus on short term needs rather than longer term architecture.

Schools can adopt a technology roadmap that will build their infrastructure over time—thus allowing them to benefit from past years investments and build more value as they continue to invest in technology, applications, devices and content.

No Child Held Back™

## NOTES

_____

_____

_____

_____

_____

_____

_____

_____

_____

_____

_____

_____

_____

_____

_____

_____

_____

YOVEL BADASH

# 11
# FLEXIBLE, OPEN PLATFORMS

**Why must the** NCHB framework be based on an open, flexible platform? More than one content provider can join. More than one education expert can make a difference. More than one technology provider can contribute. Open source is *critical* for this future. No one company, no matter how strong or wealthy they are, can solve everything. And because of the difficulty of integrating different systems, it is vital to have an integrated solution.

In the enterprise technology world and in other business areas, there is power in openness. The importance of flexibility also factors in. The NCHB framework should fit different educational organizations, provide for different issues and be able to evolve. If a school or school district implements something today, it has to be able to change tomorrow. Otherwise, we are falling into the outmoded model of NCLB; and we are, in fact, holding children back, contrary to the tenants of NCHB.

Indeed, no single technology provider can meet the requirements of every school in every district in every geographic location. Closed, proprietary education technology systems impose unnecessary limitations and *lack the flexibility* of adding new functionality whenever it is needed. Open platform systems enable schools and districts to select among potential vendors and easily customize the supporting technology infrastructure needed to meet current—and future—requirements.

What are the *benefits* of an open platform?

- Leveling the playing field and opening up avenues of contribution allows all educational stakeholders the opportunity to have a marked contribution, not only in their own communities, but literally around the world.
- Customization allows for content and communication tools to be customized meeting a particular school's or district's needs.
- Connection with community permits parents and community members easy access to school events, as well as use-friendly ways to support school fundraising and other need areas.
- Communication provides integrated, programmable applications such as text messaging, bulk mailing, and digital voice recording to communicate important information to parents and others in a school's or district's community. It also allows parents to have access to their child's assignments, test results, and other measures of progress as the tip of their fingers.
- Greater course selection gives teachers and students access to courses and course materials that are not part of their school's standard offering.
- Utilization of social media gives the school community up to the minute information on exciting happenings in the life of the school or district, increasing engagement, interest, and trust.
- Online collaboration helps students to collaborate with other students within and beyond their physical school sites. For example, a student in the U.S. can learn about Italy by communicating with an Italian student through an online discussion board. Teachers can collaborate with their colleagues to share and receive innovative approaches to teaching particular content.
- Creation of personal profiles allows students to set up their own profile, housing all of their work, assessments, and progress, so there is never any question about what has been achieved and what hasn't yet been achieved.
- Access to all classes in one place means that no longer will students have to sift through piles of paper in overcrowded bookbags that break their back. Everything they need will be online, under their unique profile.

**Highlights**

Pearson offers a free cloud-based LMS with Google App integration known as OpenClass for higher educational institutions. Pearson also offers LearningStudio, another version that can expand with the needs of individual schools.

Blackboard offers several proprietary platforms through which teachers, students and administrators can share content, communicate in a variety of ways, and students can collaborate online.

Edmodo is a network of more than 6 million students, teachers and parents. Teachers who can create lessons and quizzes for their students online while students can digitally congregate and work online. Recently, Edmodo opened their platform to third-party developers, which benefits teachers who may need direct help developing specific classroom applications.

Open platforms play right into the NCHB philosophy. They connect teachers and students like never before, allowing teachers to focus more on students' understanding concepts and less on teaching content. Open platforms also allow students to move at their own pace. Concepts like "homework" and the idea that school is just 8 a.m. to 3 p.m. are transformed into a collaborative effort any time of day anywhere teachers and students find themselves. By utilizing the power of open platforms, schools are able to customize their online needs and expand and update content for years to come.

Contrast this with the model set forth by NCLB. There is no freedom, it's not really open and teachers are directed from above. Under this model, what should be taught is determined by the federal government, the state, and the district. System standardization is the top priority and schools and districts have almost no flexibility in what they can do. Under the NCLB vision systems and technology are provided from above leaving little room for local innovation, and little room for schools and teachers to make adaptations that fit their situation.

In order to fulfill the NCHB vision, schools and districts will rely on open platforms that can *scale* in the future. They will need to have open systems that *engage* with the education stakeholders as well as the community around them. Failing to do so would lead to higher costs and the inability of schools to meet future challenges in a cost effective way.

If we truly want to create a world where no child is help back—then openness is the key!

## Already On It

Examples of open platforms for content management in education include:

Claroline—an Open Source eLearning and eWorking platform allowing teachers to build effective online courses to manage learning and collaborative activities on the Web.

Moodle—a course management system (CMS); a free, open source package designed to help educators create effective online learning communities.

Dokeos—a learning suite that allows you to create, organize, follow and coach learning activities.

NaMaYa—a cloud-based platform that is open source so that it allows each school and each teacher to adapt it to fit their needs.

Sakai—an online Collaboration and Learning Environment, support for portfolios and research collaboration.

DSPACE—an open source solution for accessing, managing and preserving scholarly works.

## Recommended Reading

*The World is Open: How Web Technology is Revolutionizing Education,* Bonk, Curtis J., 2011

*Rethinking Education in the Age of Technology: The Digital Revolution and Schooling in America,* Collins, Allan, & Halverson, Richard, 2011

*A New Culture of Learning: Cultivating the Imagination for a World of Constant Change,* Thomas, Douglas, & Seely Brown, John, 2011

## A Few Guidelines

1. What does "open source" mean to you?

2. What tools are vital on a learning platform, and what tools are non-vital?

3. What existing learning tools would you select for inclusion on your "dream" platform?

4. What value and benefit should the world's best learning platforms provide?

5. What does "open platform" mean to you?

No Child Held Back™

## NOTES

_____

_____

_____

_____

_____

_____

_____

_____

_____

_____

_____

_____

_____

_____

_____

_____

_____

**For Your Exploration**

1. Could learning extend outside the classroom, beyond the bell—and could teaching and learning still happen naturally? Why or why not?

2. Could we integrate leading-edge technologies with ideas for a world-class learning platform that would be popular amongst students, teachers and parents? How could we do this? What would such a platform be like?

3. Do you think an open platform would be useful for you as a teacher? What about for your students?

4. How do you imagine using an open platform would change the structure of your day and your practices as a teacher or parent? What would be the benefits? Any challenges?

5. Do you think an open platform would be embraced by parents and other stakeholders?

No Child Held Back™

## NOTES

_____

_____

_____

_____

_____

_____

_____

_____

_____

_____

_____

_____

_____

_____

_____

_____

_____

## Talking Points

1. Platforms need to be open from the standpoint of empowering parents, students, and teachers.

Parents, students, and teachers want to be able to influence the educational system. Open platforms with well-established boundaries allow them to do this in ways that offer a real contribution to the teaching and learning process.

2. Platforms need to be open from a technology standpoint.

If a district or school chooses a certain provider to the exclusion of others, it is limiting its teachers, students, and parents from accessing the best materials available to fit their needs and reduces the future flexibility of such a system.

3. The competitive advantage of schools should be in the quality of their pedagogy, leadership, and levels of rigor—not in content or technology.

Content can be altered and improved at any time, in any way. Pedagogy and leadership arise from human commitment, innovation, and education. This has to be cultivated. When attention and intention is focused here, schools and districts are able to compete. They have the best human beings with the best skill sets employing the best methods that allow students to thrive.

4. The total cost of ownership is much lower with an open platform than with an exclusive system.

Look at any technology area in the business world and you will find that open-source based systems are the most cost effective and in many cases support great innovation. When dealing with a closed exclusive system, the vendor can set the rules and will follow their own interests when it comes to innovation and overall advancement of the platform.

The more open and more standard a system can be the lower its long term cost of ownership. Schools need to strive to use open based platforms and content as much as possible to support future flexibility, scalability and innovation.

No Child Held Back™

**NOTES**

_____

_____

_____

_____

_____

_____

_____

_____

_____

_____

_____

_____

_____

_____

YOVEL BADASH

# 12
# CONCLUSION

**If you have** made it this far, you are no doubt inspired to achieve the NCHB vision! Can we really make this vision a reality? What will it really take?

Well, that's where you come in. Chances are, something in this book has deeply moved you.

Maybe it's the idea that everyone has a purpose to be fulfilled, and our schools can become fires that ignite the spark of passion and dream of every child and educator who walks through the door.

Maybe it's your awareness that the world truly is at our fingertips, through digital information available to us in open source platforms built on the collective strengths and wisdom of talented minds from around the world.

Maybe it's the vision that a child in a rural, poor neighborhood in northeastern North Carolina can have the same quality education as a child born into a wealthy family in the Hamptons of New York— the idea that technology and an open source framework can indeed level the playing field to become the great equalizer of our time.

Maybe it's the idea that, in a digital content rich marketplace, *you too* have something to design or teach that can touch a child halfway around the world, bringing him or her closer to actualizing his or her purpose.

Or maybe it's the idea that all education reform players can come together powerfully under one framework, aligned under a common purpose, while retaining their unique perspectives and tools.

Whatever it is that moves you, pay attention. There are no accidents. You are reading this for a reason, and that reason will be realized as you take decisive action.

Had Martin Luther King, Jr. not shared his dream, we may still be living in a world of segregated schools where citizens were judged by their color rather than the content of their character.

Had Steve Jobs ignored the nudge within him to revolutionize our device and apps/content consumption, we may still be using our phones just for voice conversation, unaware of the rich information, resources, and opportunities available to us from around the world.

Had Oprah Winfrey given up the first time she was ridiculed as a large black woman playing in—what was, at the time, a man's world —millions of women may have never come to know their worth.

You see, within each of these leaders came a moment of choice: *Should I follow the call or should I not? Is it worth it? What if it doesn't work out?* Thankfully, for us, they said yes, and impacted the quality of life for generations to come.

Right now is *your* moment. Will *you* answer the call?

While NCHB holds the potential to be global in impact, its ability to be realized happens locally, one person at a time. It is truly in *your* hands.

So, the real question is not *can* it be realized, but what *will* be realized through what only you can uniquely contribute?

I implore you: answer the call. Join the minds and hearts of millions, who just like you, will read this book and be inspired to act. Make your impact locally as a representation of this emergent global team, all aligned in a common belief that every child can thrive, and that *no* child deserves anything less than our absolute and unwavering commitment to co-create together a system that works to ignite the spark within them.

Ready. Set. GO!

The following appendices lay out ways to get started.

Don't let one more moment pass you by. Change your world!

YOVEL BADASH

# APPENDIX A:
# THE NO CHILD HELD BACK PROGRAM

**As you have** progressed through this book, you have learned about the NCHB approach, its potential impact, and tools and concepts that make it possible. No doubt you are inspired to do something to move our world forward to a place where *every* child is thriving! But just how would you go about distilling all of the resources here to something practical, manageable, and relevant for your particular school or district?

Here at the No Child Held Back consortium, which is led by NaMaYa Inc., many partners are working for change, comitted to bringing together all the best talents and initiatives in education reform. We believe that school improvement should not be limited to underperforming schools and districts, but that all schools and districts should continually strive to improve the teaching and learning process—ensuring that all children receive a high-quality education that allows each child to reach his or her full potential

To this end, we have created an NCHB *program* to allow a school or district to align itself with the NCHB *approach*. The program itself is designed to take a school to its next level of achievement, based on the school improvement continuum developed out of research outlined in the McKinsey & Company report, *"How the World's Most Improved Schools Keep Getting Better."*

## Here is how the NCHB Program works:

It occurs over three months, and includes three different phases. During the program, you will examine and take away strategies from model schools and districts that have made significant academic gains in a short period of time. You will set target goals for school improvement and design an implementation plan that will take your school(s) to the next level. You will launch your school's personalized website, employ fundraising tools, explore content creation tools and learn to utilize technology in ways that will improve communication, build community, provide exemplary content, and bring education into the 21st century in your area.

**PHASE 1:** Phase one focuses on *defining your vision*.

Whenever you embark on a journey, be it the school improvement journey or a literal journey, you need to have some basic information about both your starting point *and* your destination. In Phase 1, you will determine your "starting point" using a school/district ranking system and determine your "destination" by creating (or expanding or revising) your school's or district's vision.

According to the McKinsey report, a key component in the school improvement process is "…facilitating the improvement journey by articulation of the aspirations, objectives, and priorities of the reform program." You will need to share your vision and include all stakeholders in the improvement process to ensure your school or district achieves the best possible results from this effort. This is critical!

In order to fully benefit from the tiered approach to school improvement provided in the McKinsey report, you will need to *identify which tier* best reflects your school or district starting point on the improvement journey (i.e. poor to fair, fair to good, good to great, or great to excellent). If you are working on district-wide improvement, you may need to identify a tier for each school particularly if schools within your district vary widely in their performance and offerings. The ranking will be determined by evaluating a variety of information such as student test scores, building and site resources, parent participation levels, community involvement, and teacher-student data. You may also choose to collect additional data.

If you want to sign up for free with the NCHB program, or you just review some of the documents available to you, visit www.nochildheldback.com and follow the directions there.

**PHASE 2:** Phase two focuses on *establishing clear goals.*

During Phase 2, you will identify exactly *how you intend to make your move to the next level* of the school improvement continuum. You will be *guided to write goals that empower you and your team* to achieve measureable results. You will also *see case studies of schools* and districts that have been successful at moving up the school improvement continuum, based on results.

In order to support you in achieving your goals, during this phase of the program, you will have access to resources including:

**Data Sources**—used to help you distill hard data and collect perceptual data from the variety of stakeholders in your school's or district's community

**Creation Tools**—you will be able to explore digital communication tools, content tools, fundraising tools, community-building tools, and course creation tools to meet the unique needs of students and teachers in your school or district

**Website Creator**—you will have access to NaMaYa's website wizard, a user-friendly tool that allows you to transform the typical school Web environment from a one-way communication tool to a multidimensional platform that serves your entire educational community.

All of these tools will provide a rich set of resources allowing you to achieve extraordinary results.

**PHASE 3:** Phase three focuses on *implementing your customized action plan.*

During Phase 3, you bring your work home in real time, to real teachers and real students on the front lines of learning.

The action plan that your cohorts will put together is your roadmap to school improvement and should be seen as a living document that you refer back to and continually adjust as you begin to implement changes in your school.

You will also have access to a variety of Action Plan Templates.

By the time you complete the NCHB Program, you will have much to celebrate! You will have accomplished:

1. A vision and mission statement that includes the NCHB mindset;

2. A clear understanding of where your school stands in the improvement process (school ranking);

3. Setting school and/or district SMART goals;

4. Exploring content creation tools, content development tools, communication tools and fundraising tools;

5. Creating a web-app that will integrate and support your ongoing school improvement efforts;

6. Applying innovation and creativity to develop an NCHB Action Plan that will guide the entire school improvement process;

7. Sustainability—the opportunity to use support in implementing your action plan, keeping it going—and continuing growth after the third month.

**For more information about this Program, please visit and contact us at <u>www.nochildheldback.com</u>**

Whether you choose to use this Program or another one that aligns with the NCHB philosophy and approach, we encourage you to take decisive action toward the goal of every child excelling. The final appendix on the following pages provides yet other ways you can impact change.

No Child Held Back

**NOTES**

_____

_____

_____

_____

_____

_____

_____

_____

_____

_____

_____

_____

No Child Held Back™

## NOTES

_____

_____

_____

_____

_____

_____

_____

_____

_____

_____

_____

_____

_____

_____

_____

_____

_____

_____

# APPENDIX B:
# ACTIONS YOU CAN TAKE NOW!

*"Vision without action is a dream. Action without vision is simply passing the time. Vision in action can move the world."* —*Joel Barker*

**As you lend** your voice and talents to the team of educational visionaries around the world who are making real changes in the lives of kids, here are some suggestions for things you can do *right now*. The suggestions come from people just like you who are having great success.

Read the list that applies to you, add your own ideas, use the Statement of Committed Action on the last page of this section to commit to clear actions, a clear timeframe for taking them, and select someone who you will use as an accountability partner. Then *go do it. Go take action!* And don't forget to let us know about your progress by joining the NCHB consortium dialogue at www.nochildheldback.com.

On the following pages, find some of our suggested action items you can take or you can jot down your own. >>

**If you are a Parent, you can...**

- Create a "Greatness Discovery Journal" in which you jot down your observations of the interests and talents that seem to be emerging for your child/children. Share this with your child's/children's teacher(s) as a way to engage them in partnering with you to call forth your child's gifts.

- Organize an NCHB Book Club. Dedicate one chapter to each meeting date, and use that date to brainstorm ways that you and the other parents, teachers, and community stakeholders who are part of the Club can implement the ideas in the book. You can use the "For Your Consideration" questions at the end of each chapter to prompt discussion.

- Do an online search of "multiple intelligences" and "learning styles." Have your child take any assessments that may be on the sites. Discuss your findings with your child's teacher and ask for ways that you can team up to provide your child with learning activities that match his or her natural modes of learning.

- With your child, do an Internet search of "free online courses". See what he or she gravitates toward. Find out what your child is learning in school and how the course he/she is interested in can supplement the learning.

- Join the NCHB Consortium to share your ideas and hear about what other parents are doing in their sphere of influence. Visit: www.nochildheldback.com

- Other ideas:_____

_____

_____

- Other ideas:_____

_____

_____

_____

- Other ideas:_____

_____

_____

_____

_____

_____

_____

_____

_____

_____

_____

_____

_____

_____

_____

**If you are a Teacher, you can...**

- Share *No Child Held Back* with administrators and other teachers in your school, perhaps through a Professional Learning Community, School Leadership Team or in a faculty meeting setting. Initiate a conversation. Invite your colleagues to consider how the NCHB approach could impact your school and district.

- Do an Internet search of online content marketplaces websites and the Khan Academy videos. What is out there that would add value to the content you are teaching? What can you write to contribute to this emerging body of work?

- Do an Internet search of "multiple intelligences" and "learning styles" assessments. Use the tools that you find most valuable to assess the needs of your students. How can you alter your instructional approach with your existing resources to meet various learning styles?

- Inspire your principal and a team of teachers from your school to implement the NCHB Program outlined in Appendix A.

- Join the NCHB Consortium to share your ideas and hear what other educators are doing within their sphere of influence. Visit: www.nochildheldback.org

- Other ideas:_____

_____

_____

_____

- Other ideas:_____

_____

_____

_____

- Other ideas:_____

_____

_____

_____

_____

_____

_____

_____

_____

_____

_____

_____

_____

_____

_____

**If you are a School or District Administrator, you can...**

- Read the McKinsey Report and use the ranking tool found on the NCHB website to assess where your school or the schools in your district rank on the school improvement continuum.
  www.nochildheldback.com

- Gather a team of 4-5 inspiring educators from your school or district and do the No Child Held Back Program outlined in Appendix A.

- Incorporate elements of the NCHB approach on teacher evaluation tools, such as walkthrough evaluation forms or mid-year and end-of-year progress reviews

- Take stock of the technology resources in your building or district and conceive a plan that will allow teachers to use these resources to tap into the rich, free and low-cost digital content available in the marketplace

- Join the NCHB Consortium to share your ideas and hear what other administrators are doing within their sphere of influence.

- Other ideas:_____

  _____

  _____

  _____

- Other ideas:_____

  _____

  _____

- Other ideas:_____

_____

_____

_____

_____

_____

_____

_____

_____

_____

_____

_____

_____

_____

_____

_____

_____

**If you are a Student, you can…**

- Create a Self-Discovery Journal where you write down observations of the activities you enjoy, topics that interest you, and situations in which you feel most yourself. Share your observations with your parents and teachers and ask for their suggestions on how you can nurture your interests into a career path.

- Think about the different skills and topics you are currently learning in school. Is there an online app that can help you learn the material in a way that's exciting to you? If not, what app would *you* develop? There might just be an opportunity for you to do that! Chances are, if it would help you, it would help other students as well!

- Organize an NCHB Book Club. During each Club meeting, focus on a chapter and brainstorm ways you and your peers can help your school put into action the ideas that you think are important.

- Join the NCHB Consortium to share your ideas and hear what other students are doing in their schools and communities. Visit: www.nochildheldback.com

- Other ideas:_____

_____

_____

_____

- Other ideas:_____

_____

_____

- Other ideas:_____

## If you are a **Community Member, you can…**

- Organize an NCHB Book Club or Educational Roundtable that brings together business owners and others in the community who have a vested interest in education. Focus these meetings on brainstorming ways that you and your peers can help the schools in your area implement the ideas and access the tools discussed here.

- Be an active participant in education town halls and school board meetings. Meet with the key decision makers in your district and ask them to read this book. Follow up with them to brainstorm ways that you can help them implement the ideas and access the tools discussed here.

- Sponsor a team from the school in your area to take the NCHB Course described in Appendix A.

- Join the NCHB Consortium to share your ideas and hear what other community members are doing within their sphere of influence.

- Other ideas:_____

_____

_____

_____

- Other ideas:_____

_____

_____

_____

- Other ideas:_____

# YOVEL BADASH

## <u>Statement of Committed Action</u>

I COMMIT MYSELF to take the following actions within the following timeframe:

**Action Item**                        **Target Date**

_____      _____

_____      _____

_____      _____

_____      _____

_____      _____

_____      _____

I will share my commitment with _____
and set a plan of follow up with them so that I have someone to hold me accountable.

**Signed:**_____

**Today's Date:**_____

No Child Held Back™

## NOTES

_____

_____

_____

_____

_____

_____

_____

_____

_____

_____

_____

_____

_____

_____

_____

_____

_____

_____

_____

_____

No Child Held Back

## NOTES

_____

_____

_____

_____

_____

_____

_____

_____

_____

_____

_____

_____

_____

_____

_____

_____

_____

No Child Held Back

## NOTES

_____

_____

_____

_____

_____

_____

_____

_____

_____

_____

_____

_____

_____

No Child Held Back™

## NOTES

# No Child Held Back

## NOTES

# ABOUT THE AUTHOR

**Yovel Badash earned** his B.Sc. from the Open University in Tel Aviv. "The way it works is simple – there are no acceptance criteria –*anyone* can learn *anything* they want," says Yovel. "When you register for a course, the university sends you a large box of course materials every semester. You have a meeting with a guide once every few weeks and you literally learn alone at home. It's a very different way of learning and seeing how most of my friends learned in 'traditional' universities, I couldn't help but think –*why isn't there more of this?*" Yovel completed his degree while holding down a demanding, full-time sales and marketing position. "My degree in Computer Science and Management is a great example of how you can literally learn anything if you have great materials, some good guidance and a lot of willpower." He went on to found NaMaYa, Inc., a next-generation education platform as a service (PaaS) provider for the education sector. Yovel consults companies and organizations in the business and education sectors in his role as co-founder and president of Strategic Biz Dev, a full-service business development firm, and he is the founder of NoChildHeldBack.com, a consortium of schools, parents, teachers, technology and content providers committed to education excellence. Write to: info@nochildheldback.com